THE DEAD SEA SCROLLS

harper ✦ torchbooks

A reference-list of Harper Torchbooks, classified
by subjects, is printed at the end of this volume.

THE DEAD SEA SCROLLS

An Introduction

R.K.HARRISON

University of Toronto

HARPER TORCHBOOKS
The Cloister Library
Harper & Row, Publishers
New York and Evanston

To
CHARMIAN FELICITY
and
HERMIONE JUDITH

PREFACE

THE purpose of this book is to survey the recent manuscript discoveries from the general area to the north-west of the Dead Sea, to consider some of the theories which have been propounded concerning them, and to examine certain of the problems which have arisen in the course of academic discussion within the last few years. Whilst the treatment is of a somewhat general nature, the student has been provided with notes which will serve as a starting point for more advanced study. A short bibliography includes some of the more important contributions to the discussion of the Qumran manuscripts.

I wish to acknowledge the kindness of the Editors of *The Biblical Archaeologist* in allowing me to utilise copyright material from that journal. I am also indebted to the Delegates of the Clarendon Press, Oxford, for permission to reproduce quotations from R. H. Charles, *The Apocrypha and Pseudepigrapha of the Old Testament* (1913), Volume II. My thanks are also due to Professor R. W. Nicholls of the Department of Physics, University of Western Ontario, for his advice on publications relating to radiocarbon dating. Such translations of ancient works into modern English as appear in the book are my own.

R. K. HARRISON

Wycliffe College
Toronto, Ontario

CONTENTS

PLATES

ABBREVIATIONS

1QS	*The Rule of the Community.*
1QSa	The two columns related to 1QS.
CDC	*The Zadokite Fragment*—Code of Cairo Damascus Covenanters.
1QISa	St. Mark's Isaiah Scroll.
1QISb	The Hebrew University's fragmentary Isaiah Scroll.
1QpHab	*The Habakkuk Commentary.*
1QH	*The Thanksgiving Hymns.*
1QM	*The War Scroll.*
A.V.	The Authorised Version (1611).
R.V.	The Revised Version (1881).
R.S.V.	The Revised Standard Version (1952).
ADSS	J. M. Allegro, *The Dead Sea Scrolls* (1956).
AJ	Flavius Josephus, *The Antiquities of the Jews* (Whiston ed., 1829).
APMMM	A. Dupont-Sommer, *Aperçus préliminaires sur les manuscrits de la Mer Morte* (1950).
APOT	R. H. Charles (Ed.), *The Aprocrypha and Pseudepigrapha of the Old Testament* (1913).
BA	*The Biblical Archaeologist.*
BASOR	*Bulletin of the American Schools of Oriental Research.*
BDSS	M. Burrows, *The Dead Sea Scrolls* (1955).
BO	*Bibliotheca Orientalis.*
CBQ	*Catholic Biblical Quarterly.*
DJD	D. Barthélemy and J. T. Milik, *Discoveries in the Judean Desert I.* Qumran, Cave I (1955).
D-SDSS	A. Dupont-Sommer, *The Dead Sea Scrolls* (1952 ed., transl. E. M. Rowley).
DSSET	T. H. Gaster, *The Dead Sea Scriptures in English Translation* (1956).
DSSHU	E. L. Sukenik (Ed.), *The Dead Sea Scrolls of the Hebrew University* (1955).
DSSMM	M. Burrows (Ed.), *The Dead Sea Scrolls of St. Mark's Monastery* (1950-1). 2 Vols.

ABBREVIATIONS

GA	N. Avigad and Y. Yadin, *A Genesis Apocryphon* (1956).
HBDSS	C. Roth, *The Historical Background of the Dead Sea Scrolls* (1958).
HSDS	G. R. Driver, *The Hebrew Scrolls from the Neighbourhood of Jericho and the Dead Sea* (1951).
JBL	*Journal of Biblical Literature.*
JJS	*Journal of Jewish Studies.*
JNES	*Journal of Near Eastern Studies.*
JQR	*Jewish Quarterly Review.*
JSQE	A. Dupont-Sommer, *The Jewish Sect of Qumran and the Essenes* (1954).
JTS	*Journal of Theological Studies.*
MDSS	A. P. Davies, *The Meaning of the Dead Sea Scrolls* (1956).
MLDSS	M. Burrows, *More Light on the Dead Sea Scrolls* (1958).
NASMMM	A. Dupont-Sommer, *Nouveaux aperçus sur les manuscrits de la Mer Morte* (1953).
NRTh	*Nouvelle Revue Théologique.*
NT	*Novum Testamentum.*
OS	*Oudtestamentische Studien.*
PEQ	*Palestine Exploration Quarterly.*
PJB	*Palästinajahrbuch.*
QSP	S. A. Birnbaum, *The Qumran (Dead Sea) Scrolls and Palaeography* (1952).
RB	*Revue Biblique.*
VDJD	G. Vermès, *Discovery in the Judean Desert* (1956).
VT	*Vetus Testamentum.*
WJ	Flavius Josephus, *Wars of the Jews* (Whiston ed., 1829).
WSDS	E. Wilson, *The Scrolls from the Dead Sea* (1955).
ZFDSS	H. H. Rowley, *The Zadokite Fragments and the Dead Sea Scrolls* (1952).

INTRODUCTION

IT was in the early part of 1947 that a goatherd with the splendid name of Muhammad the Wolf, searching for one of his straying flock among the wadis above the Dead Sea, threw into a cave the stone which unexpectedly struck a jar full of papyrus scrolls and led to the most exciting Biblical discovery and controversy of our time. One hundred years previously, Constantine Tischendorf had stumbled across the Codex Sinaiticus, one of the earliest Greek manuscripts of the Bible, in an out-of-the-way monastery in the Sinai Peninsula. The Dead Sea find was even more sensational because among the contents of the jars at Qumran was a copy of the Book of Isaiah in Hebrew which could be a thousand years older than any previously known text.

It is not surprising that as the Dead Sea caves in the years following 1947 gave up more and more of their treasures and revealed the contents of a library of a Jewish sect, which lived in a nearby community at the time of Christ, scholars and amateurs alike embarked on speculation as to the relation between this community and Christianity. When the first documents were examined, there were some who were prepared at once to say that it was now clear that the beliefs of Christianity were merely echoes of those of the Qumran community, that Jesus or John the Baptist or both were members of similar brotherhoods, and that what we had thought were distinctive features of early Christian practice were in fact derived directly from Qumran.

Most scholars, however, have been cautious both about the date of the scrolls and their relationship to Christianity, particularly since nothing like a full examination has yet been possible of the mass of fragmentary materials which the caves have yielded. This has not, however, helped the ordinary interested layman to make up his mind as to the relevance of the scrolls to Christian faith and practice.

Have they anything to say, at least so far as their contents are now known, that will help us better to understand the New Testament or, for that matter, the Old Testament? What sort of people were these Qumran sectaries, when did they flourish and what happened to them? What prompted the late Professor Sukenik, Senior Archaeologist of the Hebrew University at Jerusalem, to hail the discovery of the scrolls as " one of the greatest finds ever made in Palestine "?

Any book written on the Dead Sea scrolls at this stage—and their number is legion—is bound to be of the nature of an interim report. It will be some considerable time before a final assessment can be made of the value of the scrolls, and before full answers can be given to the questions that everyone interested in the Bible and the story of Christianity will want to ask. But no better interim report could be given than this present addition to the " Teach Yourself " series. Professor Harrison has put us all in his debt by the masterly way in which he has handled the evidence. He begins by telling us the fascinating story of how the scrolls were found and how they eventually reached the experts. Then comes a full description of what the scrolls contain, followed by a reasoned assessment of their likely date. Next he deals with the relation between the manuscripts and the Old Testament, in particular with the common expectation of a coming Messiah. There is a most useful section on the character of the Qumran community compared with other religious communities of the period, and finally an invaluable chapter on the Qumran sect and Christianity. There is no doubt that this sober and scholarly appraisal of the evidence will be of immense help to many who have so far not had an opportunity to read more than an occasional newspaper or magazine article.

Professor Harrison modestly describes his book as a mere introduction to the subject and gives an extensive list of volumes for further reading together with full annotations of his sources. Most readers will, however, feel that as a concise guide to the scrolls for the unprofessional student this book could not be bettered.

WILLIAM NEIL

THE
DEAD
SEA
SCROLLs

CHAPTER I

DISCOVERING THE SCROLLS

No other archaeological enterprise of the present century has evoked such immediate and widespread interest as the remarkable series of events which culminated in the recovery and publication of what are popularly known as the Dead Sea scrolls.[1] Under ordinary circumstances a discovery of this kind would have taken a number of years, perhaps even several decades, to traverse the gap which normally exists between technical thought in any field and its subsequent popularising for the benefit of the layman. As regards Biblical archaeology this contention could be illustrated at some length from the discoveries of the present century in Egypt and the Near East. The expeditions of Chiera to Nuzu[2] and Parrot to Mari[3] are of great importance in establishing a background of historicity for the Patriarchal period, but little is known about the findings of these archaeologists outside scholarly circles. When Howard Carter excavated the tomb of Tutankhamun in 1922[4] his work received a good deal of acclaim, but despite this the splendour of the Egyptian Amarna period made little permanent impact upon the popular mind.

By contrast the attention of the public was captured almost immediately after the dramatic story of the scrolls had been told, and the widespread interest stimulated by this amazing enterprise has been maintained at a high level through its various stages. Some writers have spoken of this trend as a singular phenomenon of contemporary culture, and have sought to explain it in part as the result of modern media of communication. However, there can be little doubt that behind it also lies the natural interest of western Christianity in the historical period from which both the scrolls and the religion of Jesus Christ emerged. The possibility of some degree of relationship between the two was apparent at an early stage of the discovery, but because the implications were exaggerated by some writers, a good deal of controversy arose which served to stimulate public attention still further. Whilst the initial ardour of debate has diminished somewhat, the extent of the manuscript discoveries will make a protracted discussion of their contents inevitable. There is no doubt that long and careful study of the documents will be necessary before their historical and religious potential is exhausted.

Once the nature and importance of the manuscript material was realised, it was not long before descriptive and critical literature on the subject began to put in an appearance on both sides of the Atlantic. At the present it has reached such proportions that it is impossible for any single individual to digest all of it systematically, and there is no sign that the volume of literary productions is diminishing in any way. The resultant wide range of opinion, critical and otherwise, which has been expressed on such matters as the provenance and date of the manuscripts, their place in the history of Judaism and their relationship to Christianity, makes it clear that the present debate on the scrolls is likely to be continued for a number of years. Before this can be appreciated fully, however, it will be necessary to give some attention to those factors which have provoked such a situation.

Commencing with the early months of 1947, the rugged, inhospitable area lying to the north-west of the Dead Sea began to yield up an amazing number of manuscripts and literary fragments, some of which antedate considerably the earliest surviving Hebrew manuscripts. Different accounts exist of the manner in which the original discovery was made,[5] but according to the report of the then Director of Antiquities in Jordan, Mr. G. L. Harding,[6] the credit for this achievement, accidental as it was, r ust be given to a goatherd, Muhammad Adh-Dhib (Muhammad the Wolf), who belonged to the Bedouin tribe of Taʿamireh. Whilst searching for a straying goat near the Wadi Qumran he found a cave in the steep rock of the hillside. Throwing in a stone so as to frighten off any lurking animals, he heard a sound as of something breaking instead of the expected clatter of his stone on the rock. Somewhat apprehensively he fetched a companion, and after further effort they gained access to the cave.

There they saw several large jars standing on the cave-floor, one of which had been damaged by the stone which Muhammad Adh-Dhib had thrown in previously. Picking their way amongst other fragments of pottery they began to search eagerly for the hoard of coins which they confidently expected to find hidden in the cave. But instead of gold, they found when they examined the virtually undamaged jars that they contained some rolls of leather and papyrus wrapped in cloth. However, they realised from their appearance that these articles had a value as curios, and selecting the best they smuggled them into Bethlehem, avoiding the customs officials of the Hashemite kingdom of Jordan in the process. One merchant to whom the goatherds attempted to sell the scrolls[7] informed the Syrian Metropolitan of Jerusalem, Mar Athanasius Yeshue Samuel, of the existence of the documents,[8] in the belief that they might be ancient Syriac manuscripts. When the Metropolitan saw one of the documents, he recognised the writing on it as Hebrew rather than Syriac, and the material as either leather or parchment, but he was unable to determine the significance of the scroll. He attempted to purchase all the manuscripts which had been removed from the cave, but some time elapsed before he finally acquired five of the documents along with some other fragments, and these were stored in the Monastery of St. Mark in Old Jerusalem.[9]

Realising that these ancient writings were likely to be of considerable importance to the world of scholarship, the Metropolitan Samuel sought professional advice from the staff of the École Biblique, an eminent French Dominican institution in Old Jerusalem devoted to Biblical and archaeological study. A visiting Dutch professor, Father J. P. M. van der Ploeg, obliged the Archbishop by calling at the Syrian monastery and examining the texts, one of which he identified as a very early copy of the Book of Isaiah. On taking these tidings back to the École Biblique, van der Ploeg was assured that it was quite unreasonable to suppose that manuscripts of such antiquity were still extant, and being persuaded that the documents were spurious in nature, he abandoned further consideration of the matter for the time being. The Metropolitan was far from satisfied, however, and sought to obtain an interview with Mr. G. L. Harding, but without success. The Syrian Patriarch of Antioch whom he also consulted offered him very little in the way of guidance or encouragement in his beliefs concerning the importance and antiquity of the manuscripts, and finally the Metropolitan determined to investigate the matter himself, despite his limited knowledge of Hebrew. With the help of a Jewish journalist named Tovia-Wechsler[10] the text of the Isaiah manuscript was positively identified and seen to contain slight divergences from the Masoretic version. However, the nature and value of the remaining documents which were being examined appeared to be unrecognised.[11]

Still far from discouraged, the Metropolitan Samuel continued his search for expert opinion on the manuscripts in his possession.[12] Finally, two librarians from the Hebrew University of Jerusalem visited the monastery, and after examining the scrolls said that an expert in palaeography would need to see them before a decision on their nature and antiquity could be made. The senior archaeologist of the University, the late Professor E. L. Sukenik, was in the United States at that time, and when he returned in November 1947, he was informed by a Jerusalem dealer in curios that some manuscripts from the Dead Sea area had been acquired by another dealer in Bethlehem.[13]

In his diary for November and December of that year, Sukenik recorded the excitement which he experienced when he visited the Bethlehem dealer to examine the documents and jars in his possession. He inclined to the belief that the cave in which the manuscripts had been found had served as a *genizah*,[14] but was becoming increasingly aware of the importance and antiquity of the scrolls. On December 1st, 1947, he wrote in his diary:

" I read a little more . . . I'm afraid of going too far in thinking about them. It may be that this is one of the greatest finds ever made in Palestine . . ." [15]

Two days prior to this entry, Sukenik had managed to purchase most of the scrolls which he had examined in Bethlehem, along with two pottery jars in which the manuscripts were alleged to have been discovered. Towards the end of December 1947 he was able to acquire a very dilapidated portion of manuscript. As he studied these documents he became increasingly convinced of their immense antiquity and their unquestioned importance for Biblical study.

The Hebrew scrolls which Sukenik had purchased, and which were subsequently published posthumously in Jerusalem,[16] numbered three in all, one of which was in four sections. This latter proved to be a compilation of thanksgiving psalms or hymns, whilst the other two consisted of an imperfect copy of Isaiah and a war document. The Isaiah manuscript was much more fragmentary than the one which the Metropolitan Samuel had acquired from the Bedouin tribesmen. Whilst only approximately a dozen fragments of the earlier chapters had survived, the remainder of the prophecy from chapter forty onwards was reasonably well preserved. The War scroll proved particularly attractive in content to Sukenik at a time when Jerusalem was being shelled by Arab forces, and he gave it the provisional title of " *The War of the Children of Light with the Children of Darkness* ".[17]

All these developments were taking place at a time when the future of Palestine was hanging precariously in the balance. Since the early months of 1947 the British mandatory government had endeavoured to prevent refugees and immigrants from Europe and elsewhere from landing in Palestine. The Jews had replied to this measure by organising terrorist activities, which in turn brought reprisals from British military forces. Tension was mounting between the Arab and Jewish sections of the capital and its environs, making it exceedingly dangerous to cross from one to the other, or even to undertake short journeys outside the city such as the one which Sukenik had made to Bethlehem. On November 29th, 1947, the United Nations voted for the partition of Palestine, and the tension between Jews and Arabs increased still further. Fighting flared up intermtitently, and it was under these conditions of

open hostility that Sukenik endeavoured to obtain still more
of the manuscripts from the Bedouin Arabs who had discovered
them.

Up to this time Professor Sukenik appears to have been completely
unaware of the fact that the five other scrolls acquired by the Syrian
monastery were even in existence. A Syrian merchant indulged in
a measure of intrigue with the intention of securing the manuscripts
from the monastery for Sukenik to purchase, and although he failed
in his enterprise, he did make it possible for Sukenik to borrow some
of the scrolls for several days. He copied out a few columns from
the Isaiah manuscript in order to effect a comparison with the second
fragmentary copy of the Book of Isaiah which he himself had
acquired previously, and on Februrary 6th, 1948, he returned the
borrowed scrolls to the Syrian monastery.

Despite the tense political situation in Palestine, the Metropolitan
Samuel had been continuing his efforts to secure expert opinion on
the nature and date of the manuscripts in his possession. Finally one
of his monks, the late Father Butrus Sowmy, recalled an earlier
contact with the American School of Oriental Research in Jerusalem,
and was given permission to visit the Institution in order to explain
the nature of his mission. In the absence of the Director, Sowmy
first told the Acting Director, Dr. J. C. Trever, that the manuscripts
had been discovered in the archives of the monastery, but later
disclosed the real source' of the documents. Trever examined
them, and after comparison with the archaic script of the Nash
Papyrus[18] he became thoroughly convinced that the manuscripts
were extremely old. He copied out a passage from the Isaiah
scroll, and when he was satisfied as to the true nature of the text, he
visited the monastery without further delay and received permission
from the Metropolitan Samuel to take the manuscripts to the
American School in order to photograph them.[19]

The fighting which was in progress in Jerusalem delayed this
operation somewhat, but as soon as prints from the Isaiah scroll were
available they were sent by airmail to Professor W. F. Albright,
the eminent Biblical archaeologist of Johns Hopkins University in

Baltimore. After a brief examination of the photographs, Albright wrote by return airmail in part as follows:

" My heartiest congratulations on the greatest manuscript discovery of modern times ! There is no doubt in my mind that the script is more archaic than that of the Nash Papyrus . . . I should prefer a date around 100 B.C. . . . What an absolutely incredible find ! And there can happily not be the slightest doubt in the world about the genuineness of the manuscript . . ." [20]

When Dr. Millar Burrows, the Director of the American School of Oriental Research that year, returned from a visit to Iraq on February 28th, he also recognised the importance of the discovery. The Metropolitan Samuel was sufficiently convinced by this time to take immediate steps for the safeguarding of his treasure, and within a few days the scolls had been taken out of the country.

In the May 1948 issue of the *Biblical Archaeologist* the news of the discovery was announced to the scholarly world.[21] This created an extremely delicate and problematical situation for Mr. G. L. Harding, who up to that time had been in complete ignorance of the existence of the scrolls. He had recently been placed in charge of archaeological discoveries in Transjordan and Arab Palestine, and in this capacity he was responsible for examining the location or source of all archaeological artefacts recovered from the area under his jurisdiction. More serious still was the fact that under Jordanian law such properties belonged to the Government, so that the exporting of the scrolls without the permission of the Jordanian Department of Antiquities was a contravention of the law. Unfortunately neither Sukenik, the Metropolitan Samuel, nor the authorities at the American School of Oriental Research in Jerusalem seem to have been aware that their first responsibility under the Jordanian nationalisation law was to inform the appropriate authorities as to the nature of the discovery.[22] This placed Harding in an embarrassing position, for apart from other considerations it seemed virtually impossible for the original site to be located and examined under proper supervision.

In the meantime the political situation in Palestine was deteriorating rapidly, and became acute when the British mandate terminated at midnight on May 14th, 1948. The British forces, who had suffered considerably under the burden of mandatory rule, withdrew from Palestine at the appointed time, and this move was followed by bitter fighting between the Jews and Arabs. The latter shelled the Old City of Jerusalem in the process and caused considerable damage to the Syrian monastery. However, the scrolls had by this time reached the United States,[23] and so were out of range of the conflict. Early in 1949 the Metropolitan Samuel agreed to allow the American headquarters of the Jerusalem and Baghdad Schools of Oriental Research a period of three years in which to publish the contents of the scrolls. Apparently the Metropolitan had been encouraged to believe that this procedure would greatly increase the cash value of the documents,[24] but in actual fact the reverse proved to be the case. Once the contents of the scrolls were made public the demand for the original documents became less acute, despite the high monetary value placed upon them in certain quarters.

Facsimiles of three of the Dead Sea scrolls[25] were published in New Haven with characteristic speed and accuracy, and revealed that the five documents acquired by the monastery actually comprised only four complete scrolls, the other manuscript, which dealt with the rules of living of a particular religious community, surviving in two halves.[26] The remaining unpublished scroll had defied all attempts at unrolling,[27] and just as success in this direction appeared probable, the agreed time-limit of three years expired. The Metropolitan Samuel insisted on regaining custody of the documents forthwith.

Whilst the American scholars had been busily occupied in publishing the contents of the scrolls in their possession, the Jordanian authorities had been insistent in their demands for the return of these priceless archaeological materials. Harding himself made arrangements for a search-party to discover the precise location of the cave from which the scrolls had been recovered, and receiving little practical help from the monastery and the American School, he obtained a detachment of Jordanian troops and searched the area to the west of the Dead Sea until the original site was located near the

Wadi Qumran.[28] The presence of pottery in the first cave to be examined encouraged Harding to undertake a thorough archaeological examination of the site, despite pressing political difficulties. Two weeks after the cave had been rediscovered, a systematic excavation of the location began on February 15th, 1949.[29]

Mr. Harding, Father de Vaux from the Dominican *École Biblique*, Captain Phillippe Lippens, a Belgian United Nations observer, and Joseph Saad of the Palestine Archaeological Museum in Jerusalem were in charge of the work at Qumran, and were startled to find a great many fragments of leather, linen wrappings from which the contents had been removed, and broken pieces of jars which had apparently housed the original scrolls. Quite obviously the archaeologists had been forestalled in their search by other illicit investigators, who had left behind unmistakeable traces of their activities.[30] It was estimated that as many as fifty of the pottery containers had originally been placed in the cave,[31] which indicated that other manuscripts or fragments had been removed illegally from the cave, probably by Bedouin tribesmen towards the end of 1948.

Since some time had elapsed between the looting of the site and the organised expedition of February 1949, the difficulties in the way of recovering all the fragments which had been removed were formidable.[32] By now the Bedouin were increasingly aware of the monetary value which the fragments could command, and the financial implications of the situation were assuming serious proportions. In the end a large amount of money changed hands before the bulk of the fragments were in the possession of the proper authorities. Consequent upon exhaustive enquiries by Saad, Harding was able to locate the Bedouin tribesmen who had participated in the illegal excavations. From them he obtained the full story of the original discovery, and at the same time won their confidence in a way which was to pay valuable dividends subsequently.

As a result of excavations in the first Qumran cave some six hundred manuscript fragments representing various literary works were recovered. The small pieces of papyrus and leather which were found adhering to the soiled cloth from the cave confirmed the earlier story of the Ta'amireh Bedouin that the scrolls had been wrapped in fabric when first seen. On further examination it became apparent that the material was native Palestinian linen. The potsherds which were present in considerable quantity at the site were dated in the first century B.C. When matching pieces of the original jars were assembled they formed cylindrical vessels about twenty-six inches in height and approximately ten inches in diameter. Other smaller bowls were used as covers for the mouths of the larger jars. In addition to these late Hellenistic potsherds, the cave yielded fragments of two lamps and a cooking pot from the period of Roman occupation.[33]

The manuscript fragments represented almost every book of the Old Testament, and some of them proved to be portions of the documents originally taken from the cave in 1947, thus establishing the location with certainty and demonstrating the antiquity of the larger scrolls themselves. Fragments of the Pentateuch, *peshers* (commentaries) on some Old Testament books, and small portions of extra-canonical works written in Aramaic were amongst the more interesting of the manuscripts recovered as the result of painstaking work. The portions of Leviticus 19–22 which formed part of the collection of Pentateuchal fragments were found to have been written in Palaeo-Hebrew or Phoenician character, which some scholars took as an indication of the antiquity of these remains. Small pieces of an Isaiah manuscript which were recovered from the cave matched the imperfect Isaiah scroll which Professor Sukenik had secured for the Hebrew University in 1947.[34] The non-biblical works included fragments of the *Testament of Levi*, the *Book of Noah*, and the *Book of Jubilees*, along with collections of hymns and rules for community living.

The location of the first cave immediately raised in the minds of the archaeologists the possibility of a link with some ruins, long known as the Khirbet Qumran,[35] which were situated on a rocky plateau just to the north of the Wadi Qumran. At the beginning of the Christian era a monastic community had flourished there (*c.* 110 B.C.–A.D. 68), although the site had been inhabited at earlier and later periods. An initial exploration of the ruins was made by the official archaeological party in 1949 without tangible results, and it was only two years later that further excavation revealed the presence of artefacts of a kind similar to those recovered from the Qumran caves. These findings prompted a thorough investigation of the site, the outcome of which will be dealt with subsequently.

The acclaim with which the manuscripts from the Wadi Qumran region had been received by the scholarly world filtered down by degrees to the local Bedouin, and incited them to a more careful examination of the area from which the original scrolls had been removed. The chief reason for this burst of activity was an awareness that large sums of money had already been paid to their fellow-tribesmen for the manuscript treasures which they had surrendered. Although they themselves had no idea of what the archaic scripts signified, they were quick to realise that if similar documents could be found in other caves, large monetary rewards would be forthcoming for them also. A great many individuals were of the opinion that the cave at the Wadi Qumran was almost certainly the only one of its kind, but the practically-minded Taʿamireh, nothing daunted, began scaling the faces of the watercourses in the Wadi Qumran area and explored systematically the numerous caves which honeycombed the face of the rock. In due season their arduous labours began to be rewarded, and in October 1951, some of the tribesmen visited Saad in Jerusalem and showed him a fragment of a manuscript and a portion of a leather sandal.

Questioned by Harding and de Vaux as to the source of these discoveries, the Bedouin stated that they had been recovered from a cave located some eleven miles to the south of the first cave.[36] This new site proved to be the Wadi Murabbaʿat, and when the almost vertical rock-face was examined carefully, four caves were found near its summit. About three months after the initial visit of the Bedouin tribesmen to Joseph Saad, an official party set off for the Wadi Murabbaʿat to conduct an examination of the caves. On their arrival they found that thirty-four Bedouin were busily engaged for purely personal reasons in a clandestine excavation.

However, some of them were immediately employed on the project under official supervision, since the securing of proper labour and the transporting of supplies presented a considerable problem.[37]

The caves penetrated the cliff-face for a considerable distance, and the erosion which had produced the openings high up the wall of the Wadi had also created narrow crevices in the floors of the caves which seemed to go deep into the heart of the mountain, presenting grave dangers to unwary excavators. Added to this hazard was the inconvenience caused by the dust with which the caves were freely covered, and the real danger presented by the insecure state of the roofs in the first and second caves. Erosion appeared to have weakened the ceilings at an early period and to have produced a partial rock fall, making the possibility of a complete collapse of the roof a matter of considerable concern.[38]

Careful examination of the caves under extremely hazardous conditions revealed the existence of five distinct periods of human occupation. Commencing in the Chalcolithic period (c. 4500–3000 B.C.) they continued through the Middle Bronze Age (c. 1700–1550 B.C.), the eighth and seventh centuries B.C. and the Roman period, concluding with traces of Arab occupation. Whilst Chalcolithic potsherds and flints were recovered from all four of the caves, the most striking artefact unearthed at this level occurred in the first cave with the discovery of a wooden adze-handle, beautifully polished and fitted with leather thongs for securing the flint blade.[39] Artefacts from the Middle Bronze Age were found in the second cave, and included an Egyptian scarab of Hyksos origin. The first three caves bore traces of Iron Age occupation during the eighth and seventh centuries B.C., and from this period a papyrus palimpsest written in Phoenician characters was recovered. This document, if a genuine product of the period, is of unprecedented importance.

But by far the most interesting material came from the Roman period and was deposited most freely in the first two caves. Potsherds, metal and wooden objects, leather and various fabrics in dilapidated condition were found in profusion. A number of coins belonging to the period of the Second Jewish Revolt (A.D. 132–5) dated the occupational level accurately. Some of the potsherds were found to have been inscribed in Hebrew and Greek lettering, and along with these artefacts two Greek literary papyri in fragmentary condition were uncovered. Further evidence for the second century A.D. dating of these levels was provided in a startling manner by the discovery of some papyri written in Hebrew. They were addressed to a certain Joshua ben Galgola,[40] who seems to have been in charge of a military post at the Wadi Murabba'at, by Simon Bar-Kokhba. The latter had been conducting guerilla attacks against the occupying Roman forces from A.D. 132 to 135, and the letters appear to have been communications addressed to the partisans under his command.

In March 1952, a small expedition led by Father de Vaux and Dr. W. L. Reed of the American School of Oriental Research in Jerusalem began an organised exploration of the rugged terrain in the vicinity of the Wadi Qumran in the hope of finding some other caches of ancient documents.[41] The archaeologists were fortunate in locating a second cave somewhat south of the original one, and a third cave to the north of the first. The difficulties experienced before the excavators finally found the remains of manuscripts can be imagined from the fact that the party made well over two hundred unsuccessful soundings amongst the crevices and eroded areas of the rocky escarpment from Hajar al-Asbah to Ras Feshka, a distance of approximately six miles.

Some forty locations, either crevices or caves, yielded pottery fragments similar to those found in the vicinity of Khirbet Qumran. Not all of the recesses explored were sufficiently commodious for human habitation, and the majority seem to have been used merely for purposes of storage or cooking, as the fragments of lamps, cooking utensils and jars indicated. Whilst broken storage pottery of the Qumran variety was recovered in abundance, there was a noticeable absence of coins at the site.

Some manuscript fragments from the second cave had already been sold by Bedouin tribesmen to the Jerusalem authorities before the official excavators arrived at the scene. So thoroughly had the natives done their work that only two tiny fragments of manuscript remained at the site. Of the Biblical writings which had once been deposited in the cave, portions of the Pentateuch, the Psalms and the prophecy of Jeremiah had alone survived. Approximately forty extra-Biblical works were represented by other fragments.

Access to the third cave was impeded by the presence of huge rocks in the cave-mouth. Evidently the roof had collapsed at an earlier period, possibly as the result of seismic disturbance, thus blocking the entrance effectively and wreaking havoc upon whatever parchments had been placed for safe keeping in the cave. Consequently only very small fragments were recoverable, representing about a dozen different manuscripts. By far the most exciting discovery in this particular cave was that of two copper scrolls.[42] Located near the entrance, they had been protected by the rock-fall, and although the tightly rolled sheets of metal had become oxidised over the centuries, they had at least been preserved from other forms of damage. Because of the great difficulties involved in unrolling these scrolls without occasioning irreparable damage to the contents, a series of metallurgical tests was undertaken in the United States and Britain to determine the most effective method of unrolling the oxidised copper. Early in 1956 the rolls were specially treated and cut into strips at the College of Technology in Manchester.[43] Less than five per cent of the text was destroyed in the process, and when translated, the rolls were found to contain traditions concerning the locations of treasure-hoards.

The confidence which G. L. Harding had inspired in the Bedouin tribesmen became apparent in the way in which a steady flow of manuscript fragments arrived at the Museum in Jerusalem during 1952. In July of that year the enthusiastic Arabs unearthed another batch of manuscripts from an area to the west of the Dead Sea which to the present has defied all attempts to locate it precisely.[44] The documents which were recovered proved to be very much akin to those found in the Wadi Murabba'at. In the main they comprised Nabataean[45] and Jewish papyri dealing with business matters.

Amongst the documents brought back from the area were fragments of several Biblical books, including Genesis, Numbers and the Psalms. Of very great interest was the recovery of a fragmentary text of the Minor Prophets written on leather in Greek uncial characters, and originating about the end of the first century A.D. Fragments of the text of Micah, Jonah, Nahum, Habakkuk, Zephaniah and Zechariah were contained in the scroll. Two Greek and Aramaic documents indicated a date somewhat after A.D. 106 for their composition. At a still later period the Bedouin recovered a scroll of the Minor Prophets in Hebrew from the general area of the Wadi Murabbaᶜat.[46] This manuscript, which apparently originated in the second century A.D., consisted of the Old Testament prophecies from the middle of Joel to the end of Zephaniah, and agreed closely with the traditional Masoretic text.

During the month of August 1952, an enormous number of fragments found their way into the hands of clandestine excavators before the existence of a new cave of manuscripts, located in the remains of the Khirbet Qumran community-centre, was brought to the knowledge of the authorities. From this site thousands of fragments representing a wide variety of literary works were recovered, and an effort was made to persuade learned institutions all over the world to contribute funds so that the remainder of the cache which the Arabs had taken might be bought back. A generous financial response enabled many of the fragments to be recovered,[47] and these are now being studied by experts at the Palestine Museum in Jerusalem.

Well over three hundred literary compositions were represented by these fragments. Apart from the Book of Esther all the Old Testament writings were included, and although only small portions of each have survived, it became apparent from the remains that some canonical books occurred several times in the collection, as for example the Book of Isaiah. The great wealth of literary treasure recovered from this fourth cave also included uncanonical works such as the *Book of Enoch* and the *Testament of Levi*, along with hymnaries, commentaries, community rules and other documents.

Whilst the fourth cave was being explored at the end of September

1952, a sounding made close by revealed the existence of a fifth cave, in which were some extremely dilapidated manuscript fragments. The energetic tribesmen discovered still another cave in the Wadi, and this proved to be important because it contained mutilated portions of manuscripts which had affinity with an ancient Jewish manuscript dated between the tenth and twelfth centuries A.D. This work, which is frequently known as the *Zadokite Document*, had been discovered in the *genizah* of a Cairo synagogue and published in 1910.[48]

Subsequent archaeological activities near Khirbet Qumran in the spring of 1955 added four more caves to the original number. Unfortunately most of the resultant manuscript material is badly mutilated, and will require much patient examination before it can be evaluated properly. In his address to the annual meeting of the Palestine Exploration Fund in 1957,[49] Mr. G. L. Harding reported that yet another rocky cleft had yielded up its literary secrets to the persistent Bedouin. Somewhat north of the first Qumran cave an eleventh had been discovered early in 1956, and contained several scrolls in an excellent state of preservation, despite the fact that they had not been sealed up in jars.

A partly damaged copy of the Psalter, neatly copied out and rolled up tightly, was one of the more important manuscripts found at the site. Two copies of the Book of Daniel were recovered in good condition, to supplement several fragments of Daniel from other Qumran caves. Part of the Book of Leviticus written in a proto-Hebrew script was contained in a small scroll.

A further manuscript discovery occurred in July 1952, which whilst of lesser importance than those of Qumran or Murabba'at was nevertheless of considerable interest. In the ruins of a monastery some seven or eight miles to the north-east of Bethlehem at a site known as Khirbet Mird,[50] located almost half-way between the Wadi Qumran and the Wadi Murabba'at, were found a number of extremely interesting manuscripts. These documents are much later in date than those recovered from other sites, and have been dated between the fifth and ninth centuries A.D. The manuscripts included several letters in Aramaic and Arabic, as well as sections of a Classical Greek author. A number of Biblical fragments of Christian origin were also recovered, written in both Greek and Palestinian Syriac. The former comprised portions of uncial manuscripts of the Book of Wisdom, the Second and Fourth Evangelists and the Book of Acts, whilst the latter included some palimpsests[51] of Gospel writings in fragmentary condition, as well as portions of the Book of Joshua. An official party of excavators cleared the site in the early months of 1953 and recovered other Greek, Arabic and Aramaic fragments.

Because of the large number of caves which had been excavated and found to contain manuscripts and fragments of various kinds, some standardising of nomenclature appeared to be desirable for purposes of convenient reference. As a result, the Qumran caves have come to be designated by the Capital Q prefixed by a numeral which indicates the particular site under discussion. Thus 3Q would represent the third Qumran cave explored by the archaeologists, and from which the well-known copper scrolls were recovered. The Murabba'at caves are designated by the symbol Mu, prefixed by a numeral.

Whilst the official excavation of the Qumran area was taking place in the spring of 1949, Harding and de Vaux were attracted by the presence of ruins on a rocky plateau about a mile south of 1Q and almost the same distance from the Dead Sea. Their concern was to connect the documents which they were then excavating with evidences of contemporary human habitation in the vicinity, but after a few preliminary soundings had been taken without showing positive results, the project was postponed until a more favourable opportunity presented itself.

No further exploration of the ruins was undertaken until the end of 1951, when a party of archaeologists representing the *École Biblique*, the Department of Antiquities of Jordan and the Archaeological Museum of Palestine began a systematic examination of the site.[52] The Khirbeh or ruin was located on a shelf of rock situated midway between the sea on the east and the Wadi Qumran to the south, and had long claimed the name of Khirbet Qumran.

Nineteenth-century European travellers had noted the existence of the ruins, and one early report identified the site with the Biblical Gomorrah.[53]   In 1873 the distinguished French scholar Clermont-Ganneau explored the site, but his particular interest lay in a large cemetery situated to the east of the Khirbeh and stretching down towards the Dead Sea.   He regarded this as the principal feature of the area, and accordingly he furnished a description which recorded in considerable detail the nature of the mounds and graves, including one tomb which he himself excavated.[54]   It was left to Dalman in the twentieth century to make a correct identification of the Khirbeh, and to point out the existence of Roman remains at the site.[55]

The ruins themselves assumed an increasing importance owing to the nature of the manuscripts which had been removed so dramatically from the area.   In November and December of 1951, the archaeologists excavated the main outlines of a building which was too large for an ordinary family dwelling.   The three rooms uncovered at that time indicated an extent of floor-space suitable for a meeting-hall, whilst around the ruined walls themselves were the remains of plaster benches.   One notable feature of the site was the presence of a large water-cistern which had been linked by means of a stone aqueduct with commodious natural reservoirs further along the escarpment.[56]   Of especial importance was the discovery of an intact jar, identical in shape with the remains of those recovered from 1Q, and this fact served to link the manuscripts with the people who had inhabited the settlement in antiquity.   Further exploration uncovered charred reeds and timbers, indicating that the buildings had met a violent end.   From this first archaeological campaign it became evident that a religious community had once lived at the site, that its defunct members had been interred in the adjoining cemetery, and that the sect had been closely linked with the manuscripts from the Qumran caves.

So important were these results that a second excavation of the area was carried out in the spring of 1953,[57] and this was followed by others in 1954 and 1955.   Caches of coins found during the various campaigns furnished evidence which enabled the archaeologists to place the sect in its proper historical perspective. It would appear that the site had been occupied on a number of occasions in antiquity, beginning with the Iron Age (eighth and seventh centuries B.C.). One of the potsherds recovered from this level was inscribed in contemporary Phoenician script, and this led to the suggestion that a fortified outpost had stood on the shelf of rock in the days of Uzziah of Judah (c. 780–740 B.C.).[58]

The first major cache of coins indicated that the religious community had occupied the site from about 110 B.C. to 31 B.C., when the initial occupational period of the settlement was terminated by an earthquake.[59] An interval of about thirty years followed, and a second period of habitation by the sect appears to have lasted until A.D. 68, when according to Josephus,[60] Vespasian marched down the Jordan valley to Jericho with the Tenth Legion. Some guerilla resistance may have been offered at the site by Zealot forces, which would account for its occupation by Roman soldiery from A.D. 68 to the end of the first century. The settlement was again taken over by guerilla fighters during the Second Jewish Revolt against Rome from A.D. 132 to 135. The important strategic location of the community served the Jewish insurgents for a short time until they withdrew to the south of the Dead Sea. After this the site was uninhabited, and only in the middle of the twentieth century did it assume something of its former importance.

The painstaking labours of de Vaux and Harding have made it possible for modern eyes to see something of the nature of this ancient community settlement, which in modern writings is often described as a monastery, though this is not strictly correct. Situated on the north-west corner of the main structure was a huge defensive tower whose walls were in excess of three feet in thickness. The upper storey of the tower was connected to the lower one by means of a spiral staircase, the centre column of which has survived at foundation level. The three upper rooms of the bastion were reached through an exterior door on the south side, whereas the only means of communication between the basement rooms was of an internal nature. The tower appears to have been buttressed following the severe earthquake in 31 B.C., when it sustained damage to the eastern wall and the south-east corner.

The principal community building was approximately one hundred and twenty feet square, forming the nucleus of a complex pattern of adjacent structures. One large room situated to the south of this central building appears to have been the main refectory, adjoining which was a kitchen containing the remains of a wide variety of domestic earthenware vessels, numbering over a thousand in all. What was probably the main communal kitchen was discovered just east of the tower, where the remains of several fireplaces were excavated. Further to the south-west were four or five rooms which doubtless constituted the assembly halls of the religious community. Particularly interesting were the remains of plastered benches along all four walls of one room, indicating that it may well have been a place for meditation, discussion or prayer.

One of the first-storey rooms in this particular block seems to have been the very place in which at least some of the Qumran manuscripts had been copied out. When some curiously shaped fragments of plaster had been reconstructed by the experts of the Palestine Museum in Jerusalem, they comprised a narrow table moulded on a framework of brick. It measured about seventeen feet in length and somewhat under two feet in height, and in association with it was a proportionately smaller bench and a low platform-like structure which contained shallow depressions in the upper surface. The belief that these fragments constituted the remains of the original furniture in the *scriptorium* of the community was confirmed by the discovery of two inkwells of the Roman period, one of brass and the other of earthenware, in the same debris. The depressions in the small platform may have contained holy water for purposes of ritual purification during the copying of the sacred text.[61]

At the south-east corner of the building the archaeologists unearthed the remains of a workshop which had once contained all the tools and implements used by the members of the religious brotherhood. Facilities for smelting ore and baking earthenware were also excavated at the site, indicating that the community was virtually self-supporting. But even more important than these remains were the cisterns and conduit systems which were located in the south-east part of the main building. The remnants of a septic tank with an accompanying latrine, two cracked cisterns and several large sinks stood next to the workshop, forming part of a complex system of drains and reservoirs. The source of the water seemed to be the natural cisterns at the foot of the escarpment, and these were linked to the maze of sumps, channels and cisterns of the settlement by means of a stone aqueduct which traversed the plateau. The water thus conveyed was emptied into several huge open cisterns and a great many smaller reservoirs. The cisterns had been cut into the rock and lined with a coating of plaster. One such pool was long and deep, having fourteen stone steps at one end which gave access to the water at the various levels. These steps were found to have a crack running down the centre and continuing across the floor of the cistern into several rooms beyond. The fault was most probably the result of the earth tremor in 31 B.C., occurring at a time when the site was probably unoccupied by the brotherhood.

The upper portion of the steps had been divided into four separate sections, as though to regulate access to and from the pool itself. An analagous arrangement was uncovered in a large cistern situated near the southern wall of the main building, where the steps were subdivided into small groups and separated by a wider step. This would suggest that at least some of the cisterns were employed periodically as baptistries, since formal lustrations played a prominent part in the religious observances of the community.[62] If this was actually the case, the Qumran sect would comprise one of several such religious groups which lived in the Jordan valley at the turn of the Christian era.

Whatever may have been the ritual usage of the cisterns, there can be no doubt as to their importance for the sheer existence of the brotherhood itself. In a land where an assured supply of drinking water is seldom a happy accident of nature, an elaborate system of channelling and storage would be a virtual necessity if such a community, estimated at perhaps five hundred persons, was to survive. Since the Qumran texts mention formal ritual washings on several occasions, it would be necessary for the sect to provide an overall supply of such proportions as to meet the needs of these occasions. The complexity of the entire water system would seem to indicate that more than purely normal requirements were envisaged, but this is a matter upon which a final decision must be deferred for the present.

The potsherds recovered during the excavations at the Khirbeh[63] were instrumental in dating the historical sequences and establishing an unquestionable connection between the religious brotherhood and the Qumran scrolls. Just north of the site a number of potsherds and about thirty coins were found in a deposit of unstratified material which probably originated after 31 B.C., when the damage caused by the earthquake to the community centre was repaired. The pottery fragments were dated from the Hellenistic period, and one of them bore traces of the Hebrew alphabet, inscribed in a very poor hand. The pottery remains of the first two occupational periods of the community are difficult to distinguish, since some from level I (c. 110–31 B.C.) were used after the restoration of the building at level II (A.D. 1–68). From this second level came most of the ceramic material recovered, some of which bore inscriptions or writing.[64] When the large room situated to the south of the main building was excavated during the third season, a pantry containing over a thousand dishes stacked in piles was uncovered. Here also was found a cylindrical jar in an undamaged condition which was of exactly the same shape and pattern as those in which the manuscripts from 1Q had been concealed. The third occupational level (A.D. 68–100) contained potsherds of a kind in circulation after the commencement of the Roman period.

Another reliable witness to the different levels was found in the various coins which were unearthed during the excavations.[65] It is interesting to note that of the seven hundred and fifty coins recovered, none came from the Qumran caves. Even if the latter had been used for storage or human habitation, or both, all financial transactions appear to have been made at one point within the community structure. This has been interpreted as indicating the type of communal living reflected in Acts (4 : 32 ff.), and suggesting an espoused discipline of poverty.[66] When the site was first excavated in 1951 a coin dated A.D. 10 was discovered, and this proved to be but one of many such coins which have enabled a reasonably accurate dating of the successive occupational stages to be made. The record began at level I in the Hasmonean period during the reign of John Hyrcanus (135–104 B.C.), and continued without interruption until the time of Mattathias (40–37 B.C.), the last of the Hasmoneans.

A cache of nearly six hundred coins was found when three pottery containers were unearthed in 1955 in a room to the west of the main building. Some of these were issued under the Seleucid ruler Antiochus VII (139–129 B.C.), whilst others were of Tyrian origin, the latest being dated 9 B.C. These had evidently been concealed in the ruins of the centre prior to the reoccupation of the site by the sect at the beginning of the first century A.D.

Only one coin was found from the time of Herod the Great (37–4 B.C.), despite the length of his reign, and this contrasts curiously with the series recovered from the period of his son and successor, Herod Archelaus (4 B.C.–A.D. 6). Other coins came from the period of the Roman procurators of Judaea under Augustus (A.D. 6–14), Tiberius (A.D. 14–37), Claudius (A.D. 44–54) and Nero (A.D. 54–66). Twenty-three coins of Herod Agrippa I (A.D. 37–44) were also included with these deposits, thus providing a continuous historical record up to the time of the First Jewish Revolt (A.D. 66–70). Other coins proceeded from the period after the fall of Jerusalem in A.D. 70, whilst about a dozen were dated in the Second Jewish Revolt (A.D. 132–5), and came from level III.

The necropolis which was adjacent to the Khirbeh and which had attracted the attention of Clermont-Ganneau at an earlier period, was also the object of some scrutiny by the archaeologists during the excavations at Khirbet Qumran. The graves numbered about one thousand in all, and were laid out in parallel lines extending north and south. The last feature had intrigued Clermont-Ganneau, who had noted that Islamic burials were generally oriented east and west, leading him to suggest a pre-Islamic date for the cemetery.[67] When de Vaux opened various graves, he found, as Clermont-Ganneau had done, that they were unelaborately constructed, consisting of a shaft sunk into the marl to an average depth of five feet. A small mortuary chamber was then hollowed out under one of the long walls of the shaft, after which the body was laid face upwards, usually with the head to the south, without first being placed in a coffin. The funerary chamber was then sealed by means of bricks or stones, and the trench was filled in to complete the interment.

The ceramic material frequently employed as fill for the graves was of the same general type as that found in 1Q and in the remains of the principal community building, a fact which demonstrated still further the connection between them. Whilst some of the graves were marked at the head and foot by means of a single block of undressed stone, the majority were indicated by a simple oval of pebbles. The austerity of the sect appears to be indicated by the complete absence of funerary offerings or ornamentation of the corpses.[68] Most of the skeletal remains which were recovered by de Vaux were in a poor state of preservation, but were sent to Paris for examination by Professor H. V. Vallois of the *Musée de l'Homme*, who reported that some of the fragments were from female skeletons.[69] All of the remains were those of adults, and there are no indications that children were ever interred in the cemetery.

The outcome of the circumstances surrounding the manuscripts which the Metropolitan Samuel had taken to the United States in 1949 may well furnish a fitting conclusion to the present chapter. Whilst the scrolls were being prepared for publication in New Haven, the Metropolitan was bitterly assailed by the Jordanian government for removing the manuscripts from the country without first receiving official permission, and was threatened with punishment should he ever return to Jerusalem. In reply the Archbishop urged that when he left Palestine the British mandate had already expired, and that there was then no established legal body to regulate and enforce nationalisation procedures.[70]

In addition, he stated that any money which was realised from the sale of the documents in his possession would be used for the expansion of religious and educational facilities in the Syrian Orthodox Church, since the scrolls which he had were to be considered Church property.[71] Whatever hopes the Archbishop had entertained of realising considerable sums of money from the publication and sale of the manuscripts were slow to mature. A number of American institutions of learning contemplated the purchase of one or more of the scrolls, but the questions which arose about the legality of purchasing them deterred serious efforts to acquire these four important documents.

When it became evident that the publication of their contents had effected a depreciation in the monetary value of the scrolls rather than the opposite, as had been expected, the Archbishop and his Trustees set about devising means of disposing of the documents without further delay. It was decided to advertise them in the " Miscellaneous For Sale " columns of the *Wall Street Journal*,[72] in the hope that they would be disposed of quickly and profitably. That summer, Dr. Yigael Yadin was visiting the United States, and was shown the advertisement. Using an intermediary he began negotiations for their purchase, and ultimately acquired them for a sum reported to be some two hundred and fifty thousand dollars.[73]

Finally on February 13th, 1955, Premier Sharett announced that the State of Israel had acquired the Dead Sea manuscripts which had originally been in the possession of the Syrian monastery.[74] He further stated that the government intended to erect a special museum to house these documents as well as those which Professor Sukenik had acquired for the Hebrew University in 1947. The new edifice would be named the Shrine of the Book, and would also serve as the repository for other ancient documents. After eight hazardous and troubled years the Dead Sea Scrolls were finally to be housed under one roof.

CHAPTER 2

THE SCROLLS AND
THEIR CONTENTS

ONE of the more interesting features connected with the discovery of the Qumran manuscripts was that for the most part they had been preserved in earthenware jars. Although the pottery containers from 1Q had sustained considerable damage due to the marauding activities of the Bedouin tribesmen, a reconstruction from the abundant sherds excavated at the site showed that the jars were cylindrical in shape, measuring on the average two feet in height and a foot in width.[1] The discovery of one such jar at Khirbet Qumran in an undamaged condition as well as scores of similar containers in nearby caves made it clear that these earthenware jars were employed for normal culinary purposes in everyday living, and were not specially designed to hold the scrolls, as was originally thought.

Jars of this kind had been in use for many centuries prior to the Christian era as receptacles for storing a wide range of commodities. The practice may have originated in Egypt during the Old Kingdom period (c. 2700–2200 B.C.), when the embalmers began to deposit the vital organs of the body in canopic jars, which in turn were placed beside the mummy at burial. In any event it became customary in the ancient Near East to store valuables in such containers, which may well have furnished the equivalent of a private safe.[2] The Book of Jeremiah records that the purchase-deeds of a piece of property near Jerusalem were sealed up in this manner:

" Thus says the Lord of Hosts, the God of Israel : Take these deeds, both this sealed purchase-deed and this open deed, and put them in an earthenware vessel that they may survive for an indefinite period." [3]

Literary compositions which were intended for posterity were generally deposited in jars and sealed up with a covering of pitch. Some idea of the procedure followed towards the commencement of the Christian era may be gleaned from a reference to the practice in a pseudepigraphical work entitled *The Assumption of Moses*. In this composition, as Moses delivered his writings to Joshua and instructed him concerning their preservation he spoke as follows:

> " Receive thou this writing that thou mayest know how to preserve the books which I shall deliver unto thee : and thou shalt set these in order and anoint them with oil of cedar and put them away in earthen vessels . . ." [4]

Those who deposited the Qumran scrolls probably followed an ancient practice by wrapping them in several folds of native cloth before sealing them up in the jars. Cedar-oil or other preservatives of a resinous nature may have been employed in the process of storing the manuscripts, as would seem to be indicated by the condition of the linen coverings found in 1Q.[5]

Whatever precautions may have been taken in antiquity for the preservation and survival of the Dead Sea Scrolls, they could scarcely have been expected to withstand the ravages of almost two millennia. The caves presented physical conditions almost totally removed from the ideal situations encountered in carefully prepared burial chambers located deep in the heart of a pyramid or the rock-face of a secluded Egyptian valley. Most of the caves excavated yielded traces of human or animal habitation at widely differing periods, and the damage caused by such interference was greatly augmented by the havoc wrought in different caves when rockfalls occurred as the result of seismic disturbances. The whole enterprise of excavation and recovery was one of great difficulty and danger, and those who were responsible for its success over a period of years have made a remarkable contribution to Biblical studies, for which the world of scholarship will be deeply indebted for years to come.

The sheer physical effort of endeavouring to recover pieces of manuscript amidst clouds of choking white dust was complicated

continually by the extremely fragile nature of the documents themselves. When 1Q was being excavated, the operation was carried
out under very difficult conditions, which required that only tweezers
and a camel-hair brush be employed in the process of recovering the
scraps of manuscript, lest further dilapidation or damage should
result. When the various sites had at last been cleared, the manuscript fragments were carefully packed up and taken to the Palestine
Museum where they were prepared for further examination. In
many instances the fragments were thoroughly dehydrated and
covered with a coating of white marly dust. Before they could
be examined it was necessary for them to be hydrated and cleaned,
a procedure which frequently called for a good deal of care.[6] Dr.
F. M. Cross has described the initial stages of such a task admirably:

" The first steps in preparing the manuscript are quite unex-
citing. The humidifier and the camel-hair brush are the chief
pieces of equipment necessary, and patience the sole resource
required by the scholar. Brittle, crinkled fragments are softened,
and flattened between glass plates, first of all; then comes the
delicate task of cleaning marly clay from the surface, and in some
cases from the very pores of the leather or papyrus. Some of
the fragments are extremely friable, so that to clean off the clay
is to strip off the ink of the script as well. Others crumble at the
touch of the brush unless backed with tape. Yet others have
turned black in the process of time through the action of air and
moisture. In the worst cases, a non-acid oil must be used to
reveal the script on the deteriorated surface of the leather.
Fortunately, the carbon ink used on the fragments responds well
to infra-red rays ; and fragments illegible to the naked eye are
frequently decipherable on infra-red photographs." [7]

Once the fragments recovered from the various sites had been
cleaned, they were photographed and classified as to language and
content. Whereas it was comparatively simple to identify the
Biblical fragments since the text was already familiar, the non-
Biblical manuscripts presented greater difficulties, which persisted

until some affinity with an extant work was recognised. When manuscript fragments had been identified they were placed on glass plates in the " scrollery " of the museum, and as related portions of papyrus or leather were discovered, the manuscript began to assume something of its original form.

Work of this nature is necessarily slow and often tedious. Much exhausting and painstaking labour is required before even limited success in the assembling of cognate fragments is assured. The entire process imposes exacting physical and mental stresses upon those who engage in the work, a fact to which the international team of scholars concerned with the collection and publication of the manuscript material can amply testify.[8]

The problem of according suitable designations to the major manuscripts which had been recovered from the Qumran caves arose when variant styles of reference came into existence. Whilst it was often convenient to mention a document by its tentative title, it soon became apparent that some uniformity of description would be a distinct convenience in making reference to the various manuscripts. Accordingly a system was developed which related the particular document to the site from which it had been removed. The Isaiah scroll which had been purchased by St. Mark's Orthodox Convent in Jerusalem was designated 1QISa, and as such was distinguished from the fragmentary Isaiah scroll acquired by Professor Sukenik, which was described as 1QISb. The " Manual of Discipline " or " Rule of the Community " became known as 1QS,[9] whilst the Habakkuk Commentary was styled 1QpHab.[10] The Thanksgiving Hymns and the Military scroll were represented respectively by the symbols 1QH and 1QM.[11] Subsequent references to these manuscripts in the present work will follow this general pattern.

As a result of the excavations undertaken early in 1949 by the official party, over six hundred fragments of manuscript material were recovered from 1Q after a good deal of painstaking labour.[12] Some of these tattered parchments were actually salvaged from the dump which the energetic Bedouin had made whilst they were engaged in their own clandestine treasure-hunt. The mass of fragments included small sections of the scrolls which had been removed in 1947 at the time when the cave was first discovered. The recognition of the connection between the scraps and the parent documents established the authentic nature of the latter. Of the Biblical books represented by the cache, portions of the Pentateuch and Judges were identified, along with tattered pieces of Aramaic extra-canonical writings and a few *peshers* or commentaries.[13]

Some Pentateuchal fragments consisting of several brief citations from Leviticus 19-22 had been copied in the old Hebrew or Phoenician script which was used for some centuries prior to the adoption of the square Aramaic characters towards the end of the third century B.C. This provoked questions as to the date and provenance of the fragments, and after some consideration de Vaux assigned the parent manuscript to the fourth century B.C. Albright, on the other hand, held that the fragments had been written in what amounted to a professional archaic script[14] which may well have enjoyed a tradition of usage extending over at least three centuries.

Of the apocryphal works which were recovered in fragmentary condition from 1Q, the *Book of Noah*, the *Testament of Levi* and the *Book of Jubilees* were readily identified. The latter proved to be of interest because it was written in Hebrew, and as such it raised once again the problem as to the original language of the book. According to Charles[15] the *Book of Jubilees* was compiled from earlier traditions and written in Hebrew by a Pharisaic author between the years 153 B.C. and 105 B.C. C. C. Torrey, however, maintained that the book in its original form had been written in Aramaic, and regarded the Qumran fragments as a good example of what he called " inter-Semitic translation ".[16] As matters stand at the present, any judgement as to the nature of the original language of the book based mainly on the fragments of the *Book of Jubilees* from 1Q would be somewhat precipitate.

At this juncture a more detailed consideration of the documents which were removed from 1Q by the Ta'amireh tribesmen in 1947 must be undertaken, since no manuscripts discovered subsequently are in any way comparable in importance and value for the

Biblical student. Of these documents the most sensational was the large Isaiah scroll (1QISa) published by the American Schools of Oriental Research. Surprisingly well preserved, the manuscript consisted of fifty-four columns of clear Hebrew script written on seventeen sheets of leather sewed end to end.[17] When unrolled it measured twenty-four feet in length and was approximately one foot wide.[18] The text averaged twenty-nine lines to each column, and instead of being divided into chapters and verses in the modern fashion, the prophecy was set out in clearly marked sections and paragraphs. Whilst there is frequently a general measure of correspondence between the larger divisions of this arrangement and the chapters of modern Bibles, it is by no means uniform.

Despite the fact that the scroll had obviously received a good deal of handling in antiquity to the point where repairs to the skin had become necessary, there are only ten lacunae in the manuscript and about a dozen minute holes, making restoration of the text comparatively free from difficulty. The script was suspended from faintly ruled lines, many of which subsequently disappeared, and when the original ink faded, the script was restored by re-inking the illegible portions. Scribal errors were corrected in a variety of ways, and the work of several different hands is evident in a few instances in the text.[19] A series of curious marginal symbols of an unfamiliar nature may have been intended to divide up the prophecy into sections for liturgical or devotional purposes, though in the last resort their meaning is somewhat indeterminate.[20]

The scroll of Isaiah which had come into the possession of Professor Sukenik was in fragmentary condition, and had deteriorated considerably with the passage of time. The outside of the manuscript was smeared with a coating of tacky decayed leather, and the entire document was so tightly rolled that at first it was impossible to determine the nature of the contents.[21] When the scroll was finally opened it was found to consist of one large piece and a number of lesser fragments. Such had been the ravages of time that many of the columns of scripture were only legible in infra-red photography. After completion of this rather delicate operation it became evident that the small portions contained passages from the earlier chapters of the prophecy, whilst the larger section of manuscript comprised the last third of the Book of Isaiah, with some gaps in the text.[22]   When assembled in the form of four sheets, the two smaller ones averaged ten inches in length by six inches in width, whilst the larger ones measured approximately eighteen inches in length and eight inches in width.[23]   Sukenik noted that the text of his scroll approximated more closely to the readings of the Masoretic text of later manuscripts, unlike the copy of Isaiah which the Metropolitan Samuel had acquired.

The manuscript which was by far the most beautifully and clearly written was that which contained the Commentary on the Book of Habakkuk (1QpHab).[24]   The document consisted of two pieces of parchment sewed together, and had originally measured about five feet in length and an average of seven inches in width.[25]   Traces of rulings for lines and columns were evident on the surface of the manuscript, and the letters were suspended from the lines as was the case with the other scrolls.   An unfortunate deterioration or mutilation of the leather at the bottom extended throughout the length of the scroll, with the result that several lines of the text have been lost from each column.   The beginning of the manuscript was defective, but apparently only to the extent of one column. So careful and accurate was the copyist that very few corrections were evident in the manuscript.   His characters were somewhat larger than those of 1QISa, and because the ink had been preserved with virtually no deterioration over the centuries, the script was bold and clear, making for comparatively easy reading.   Only the first two chapters of Habakkuk as found in the Masoretic text had survived in the Commentary, presumably because the third chapter, which is really a psalm, was not suited to the exegetical purposes for which the document was originally compiled.[26]   The method followed by the commentator was that of citing short sections of the prophecy, which were then explained eschatologically or allegorically in terms of the history of the religious sect from which the Commentary had proceeded.[27]

The Commentary appears to divide up the Masoretic text of Habakkuk into five major sections as follows:

(a) Social and religious inequalities (Hab. 1 : 1-5).
(b) Subjugation of the nation by a foreign power (Hab. 1 : 6-17).
(c) The Righteous Teacher and his followers (Hab. 2 : 1-4).
(d) The Wicked Priest and his party (Hab. 2 : 5-17).
(e) Divine retribution on idolators (Hab. 2 : 18-20).

Certain quite well attested interpretative principles of the ancient Jewish *midrashim* or expositions have been detected in the Qumran Habakkuk Commentary. Cryptic, allegorical and eschatological references were reinforced by such devices as the mechanical re-arrangement of letters in a word, the interchanging of similar letters, and the division or abbreviation of particular words.[28] After a short passage of Habakkuk had been quoted, the commentator followed it immediately by the term *pishro*, i.e. " its interpretation is ", or some equivalent expression. The subsequent comments were not so much an attempt to elucidate the meaning of the Biblical text as to point out the existence of certain conditions in the sect from which the document originated. The following citations will illustrate the method adopted:

(Hab. 1 : 4) *So the law has fallen into desuetude* . . . the interpretation of this is that they have rejected the Torah of God . . .

For the wicked beset the righteous . . . this means that the " righteous one " is the Righteous Teacher[29] and the " wicked one " is the Wicked Priest . . .

(Hab. 1 : 6) *For behold, I am arousing the Chaldeans* . . . this interpretation refers to the Kittim, who are swift and formidable in battle, bent on the destruction of peoples . . .

(Hab. 1 : 13b) *Why do you countenance traitors and remain silent when the wicked man confounds someone more righteous than himself* . . . this refers to the house of Absalom and their associates who maintained silence when accusations were brought against the righteous Teacher, and did not assist him against the liar who rejected the Torah in the presence of their entire congregation . . .

The Wicked Priest and the ruthless Kittim represented the spiritual and temporal opponents of the religious group for whom the Commentary had been written. The interpretation which was placed upon the words of Habakkuk was such as to lend a formal characterisation to the general nature of the spiritual and material opposition encountered, perhaps at different periods, by the Qumran sectaries. Whilst specific historical occasions or personalities need not be implied by this form of commentary, they are certainly not precluded.[30]

When the experts of the American Schools of Oriental Research received the document first entitled the " Manual of Discipline ", but more properly referred to as the *Sectarian Document* or the *Rule of the Community* (1QS), it was found to be in two portions, each of which was rolled up separately. When they were joined they constituted a scroll made up of five sheets of parchment stitched together. The overall length of the document was approximately six feet, whilst the width averaged nine and a half inches. The beginning of the manuscript had been lost, but on the basis of careful calaculation it was estimated that the original scroll had been at least seven feet in length.

The text exhibited a remarkably clear script, and afforded little if any indication of wear through handling such as was evident in the large Isaiah scroll (1QISa). The state of preservation of the Hebrew was all the more remarkable in view of the extremely brittle nature of the document when it was first discovered. The contents were written in columnar form in the usual manner, and the style of writing was not greatly different from the work of the scribe who copied out 1QISa. The text of the *Rule* consisted of eleven columns of Hebrew, with an average of twenty-six lines to each column. One or two lines from the bottoms of most columns had been eaten away by white ants, but otherwise there was no damage to the text apart from the lack of an original title. Amongst some of the manuscript fragments subsequently acquired by the Palestine Museum were two almost complete columns of text which appeared to come from the *Rule of the Community* manuscript, and which in consequence have been designated 1QSa. The end of the second column had sustained damage, and so it was impossible to tell whether or not the two documents when joined would have formed a consecutive narrative. Furthermore, there is considerable doubt as to whether the first column actually marked the commencement of the entire document.[31]

The *Rule of the Community* is by far the most important source of knowledge concerning the nature of the religious community (*yaḥad*) at Qumran. It consisted of a group of priests and laymen who lived a communal life in strict dedication to God. The scroll opened with a statement of what would be required of those seeking to " enter into the Covenant ",[32] and this was followed by the liturgical form of initiation.[33] From the *Rule* it is evident that each member of the community was required to renew his pledge of obedience annually,[34] and at this time he was reminded of those defects which would result in exclusion from the ranks of the brotherhood.[35]

The middle of the third column of the Hebrew text contained a section dealing with the nature of man and recounting the origin and destruction of sin.[36] The fifth column marked the beginning of the rules which governed community organisation proper, and with this list,[37] which occupied five full columns, the manuscript was complete, save for a concluding devotional psalm.[38]

The *Rule* indicated quite clearly that the community members were strongly influenced by apocalyptic or eschatological considerations in that they, the true Israel, were awaiting the establishing of the Divine rule on earth. Until this expectation became a reality, the sect followed an organised existence under the leadership of elders and priests, engaging in constant Biblical study and indulging in a sacramental type of worship.

The *Thanksgiving Hymns* (1QH) were in four separate portions when Sukenik acquired them. The first three of these were bundled up together in a rather casual fashion,[39] whilst the fourth section frustrated all attempts at unrolling for some time. In the main the leather on which the Hymns had been written had withstood the ravages of time and nature quite well, though portions of the document were in an advanced stage of deterioration, and only became legible after infra-red photography. When the four sections of the scroll were finally assembled they indicated that the document in its original form had comprised fifteen columns[40] of an average height of twelve inches, and containing up to thirty-nine lines of script in a column. When first compiled the scroll was probably about seven and a half feet in length.[41]

The script in which the Hymns were written approximated in size to that of 1QISa, but the calligraphy revealed that two scribes had co-operated in the work of copying out the scroll and the correction of some errors of transcription.[42] The collection of Hymns numbered about twenty in all, and reflected the traditions of the Qumran community. The majority of the compositions commenced with an ascription of personal thanks to God, and their subsequent content exhibited many points of contact with the Biblical Psalms, especially in the matter of the personal relationship existing between the worshipper and the Deity. The Hymnary appears to reflect two distinctive types of liturgical writing which gained currency some two centuries or more before the Christian era. These were the "Thanksgiving" hymns commencing with a note of thankfulness to the Deity, and the "Benedictory" compositions in which a formula of blessing opened the psalm. Despite an obvious dependence upon the Hebrew and Ugaritic literary tradition, these poetic writings were probably the most original expressions of the religious group which lived in the Qumran area.

Two short excerpts from the Hymns will serve to illustrate the character of the poetry:

"I am thankful to you, Lord,
for you have not forsaken me though I am living
as a temporary resident amongst an alien nation,
(*nor*) judged me according to my wrongdoing . . .
but you have rescued me from destruction . . ."[43]

A typical psalm of Benediction commenced as follows:

> " You are blessed, Lord,
> because you have not abandoned the orphan nor
> abhorred the poor . . .
> Your power (*is boundless*) and your glory is im-
> measurable . . ." [44]

Some scholars have inferred that the Righteous Teacher was the author of at least some of these compositions because of the reference in one Hymn[45] to a teacher of the Law who was beset by many enemies.

Probably the document whose contents were awaited with the greatest impatience was the last of the four scrolls originally purchased by the Archbishop Samuel and taken by him to the United States in 1948. This manuscript had foiled all attempts at unrolling, and just as preparations for this exacting task were well in hand, the agreed period during which the American scholars were to have custody of the scrolls expired. Because the Archbishop Samuel was at that time increasingly concerned about the depreciating value of the manuscripts, he insisted on regaining possession of all four of the scrolls.[46] It was only when they arrived in the State of Israel in 1954 that a successful effort could be made to unroll and decipher the document.

On examination it proved to be in a bad state of preservation, and required all the skill and patience of Professor J. Biberkraut to bring the operation of unrolling and reconstruction to a successful conclusion.[47] From the general condition of the document it appeared to have been exposed for a considerable period of time. There is some doubt as to whether it was ever in an earthenware container, and from the ravages of climate and the damage caused by insect pests it seems probable that the scroll had been lying on one side on the ground at some point prior to its recovery.[48] Understandably enough, its dilapidated condition was not improved by being housed under widely differing conditions of temperature and humidity, and by being transported from one country to another over a seven-year period before finding a permanent resting-place.

The poor state of preservation became abundantly evident when the unrolling was completed, for deep holes and crumbling, rotted areas were seen to be widely distributed, especially on one side of the leather roll. Because of the physical difficulties involved, the process of deciphering the columns of the document was much more protracted than had been expected at first. In consequence a preliminary report on the contents of the scroll was issued in 1956,[49] which brought before the scholarly world the long-awaited information as to its nature.

Whilst the scroll had been in the custody of the American scholars, Trever had examined a detached fragment of the manuscript, and from a reference to Lamech and his wife Bat-Enosh he had concluded that the scroll was the long-lost apocryphal *Book of Lamech*.[50] Because of this opinion the document had become familiar to scholars by that title,[51] and it was only in 1956 that the actual facts concerning the contents of the scroll became known. It proved to be an Aramaic version of several early chapters from the Book of Genesis, dealing in paraphrase form with the lives of the Patriarchs, and distinctly reminiscent in nature of the familiar apocryphal work *The Book of Jubilees*.[52] The mention of Lamech was thus quite obviously incidental to the larger purpose of the composition, which was to present a paraphrase of certain selected chapters of Genesis, following the pattern of the apocryphal writings.[53]

The preliminary report dealt principally with the last three columns of the manuscript (which were quite well preserved by comparison with the remainder); with the fourth column from the end which narrated incidents from Genesis 12, and with the second column which included the Lamech reference, and was therefore published because of the interest originally stimulated in this connection. The scroll itself had been prepared in much the same manner as the other Qumran documents. The writing was inscribed on the hair side of the skin beneath ruled lines in a clear hand similar to that of the Military document, with good word-spacing and a remarkable freedom from transcriptional errors. There were four sheets to the manuscript in the first instance, and although the beginning and end of the text were missing, it was still possible to estimate the size of the whole document. Whilst the sheets, which were held together by fine diagonal stitching, were not uniform in length,[54] they indicated that the original scroll measured approximately nine feet in length and one foot in width. An unusual method of manuscript preparation consisted of an alternating series of leather strips and blank spaces, whilst a sheet of thin white material covered the lower portion of Columns X to XV, thereby obscuring the script. Whether this supplementary substance was intended to reinforce or protect the leather at a weak or damaged section is not as yet apparent.

Professor Biberkraut reported that the ink on the scroll had apparently contributed to the process of deterioration. In certain areas it had reacted on the leather to produce a blurring of letters in the text, whilst in other places the leather had been eaten away completely, resulting in the appearance of holes in the scroll. Whilst the composition of the ink has not been investigated fully as yet, it would appear that some particular ingredient produced an acid reaction when in contact with the leather. This process may have been encouraged by hurried or indifferent preparation of the scroll itself.

A brief survey of the contents of those sections published to date indicates that in Column II, twenty-six lines were preserved from a passage containing a first-person narrative related by Lamech. In this he questioned his wife Bat-Enosh concerning the paternity of his son Noah, and then went to his father Methuselah to seek a celestial verdict upon the matter from his deceased ancestor Enoch.[55] Columns XV and XVII described the division of the earth amongst the sons of Noah, whilst the fragmentary Column XVIII dealt with Abram at Ur and Haran. The most complete columns were the last four (XIX to XXIII), of which the first two explained the reason why Abram required Sarah to conceal her identity before Pharaoh[56] and the events which followed when she was received into the royal household.[57] The remaining columns narrated the journeys of Abram in Canaan, the war of the four kings (cf. Gen. 14), and their defeat.[58]

The Military scroll, sometimes known as the *Rule of War*, was published by Sukenik under the title of *The War of the Sons of Light with the Sons of Darkness.*[59] Apart from some deterioration of the lower edge the scroll was almost entirely preserved, and was the only one to possess its outer wrappings. When unrolled the manuscript was more than nine feet in length, and somewhat in excess of six inches in width. The text was written on four sheets in eighteen columns, with the remains of another column from a fifth sheet completing the document. The writing was clear and methodical, being most akin to the Genesis Apocryphon script of any of the Qumran manuscripts.

Decomposition of the scroll had produced characteristic lacunae which were to be found principally in the second portion of the document. The position of some of these gaps made a tentative reconstruction of the text somewhat less difficult than had been imagined at first, whilst a few detached fragments when fitted into their proper places expedited matters still further.

The scroll dealt in an eschatological fashion with the conduct of a military operation between the " Sons of Light ", consisting of the tribes of Levi, Judah and Benjamin, and the " Sons of Darkness ", who comprised the enemies of Israel and included the Philistines, Greeks, Edomites, Moabites and Ammonites. A short prologue spoke of the coming conflict, and this was followed by a list of directions for battle, and the prayers and thanksgivings which the " Sons of Light " would pronounce at different times.[60] Some scholars have seen in this manual a reflection of the military struggles between conquering Israel and the Canaanites of the days of Joshua,[61] whereas others have recognised some degree of correspondence with Roman methods of military procedure.[62] However, it does not seem either possible or desirable as yet to decide whether an actual conflict or an apocalyptic Armageddon was being envisaged when the document was compiled.

The fragments of Daniel which were recovered from 1Q and acquired by the Archbishop Samuel were three in number, and were described by Professor G. E. Wright as follows:

" In the matted mass of leather fragments were three sections from Daniel in addition to several fragments from some other piece of Hebrew religious literature. Interestingly enough, the three fragments of Daniel are from two different scrolls. Two pieces are paleographically near the Isaiah scroll while the other is very similar to the Habakkuk script. Two pieces are from the same column and contain portions of Daniel 3 : 23–30 in Aramaic, whilst the third fragment contains portions of two columns : Dan. 1 : 10–16 and Dan. 2 : 26 (including the point where the Aramaic of Daniel begins). One of the pieces of the passage from Dan. 3 : 23–30 measures 4 by 4½ in., and its companion from the same column is 2½ in. square. Together they show that the column must have been almost 6 in. wide. The other fragment measures 5½ by 3 in., and the columns were apparently less than 4 in. wide . . . The text is substantially the same as that of our current Hebrew Bible (the Masoretic text). The chief differences, like those in the Isaiah manuscript, have to do with the spelling of words." [63]

A brief survey of the fragments found in the other caves of the Wadi Qumran may be undertaken at this juncture. From 2Q were recovered nearly two hundred scraps of manuscript, which were purchased by the Palestine Museum and the École Biblique. The canonical writings represented by this cache included short sections of Jeremiah, Ruth, the Psalms and some Pentateuchal books. Of the latter, a fragment of Leviticus in Hebrew similar to the one recovered from 1Q proved to be interesting because of the early form of script in which it was written. Non-Biblical texts formed a significant proportion of the fragments in the cave, and were for the most part eschatological, apocalyptic or Messianic in nature. A small portion of the Book of Jubilees in Hebrew was similar in character to the Jubilees fragment unearthed in 1Q.[64]

The third Qumran cave, situated a little over one mile north of 1Q, housed a remarkable cache of manuscripts. Access to the fragments was difficult because the cave roof had collapsed in antiquity, but in the end several hundred mixed scraps of manuscript were recovered. Remnants of Biblical books included small sections of a commentary on the first few lines of Isaiah, with fragments of Lamentations and perhaps of Genesis also, though the latter are somewhat doubtful. Apocryphal manuscripts were represented by dilapidated portions of hymns, a sectarian manual, and several apocalyptic texts in both Hebrew and Aramaic.[65] By far the most significant discovery in 3Q was that of two copper scrolls which had escaped destruction when the remainder of the cache sustained damage in antiquity.[66] One of these scrolls was in two portions, and originally all the strips appeared to have been riveted together, forming a metallic sheet about eight feet long and one foot wide. The script had been beaten into the metal surface and faced inwards when the long strips were rolled up. The copper was completely oxidised, a fact which presented enormous technical difficulties in the way of unrolling the documents. Before this was finally achieved, Professor Kuhn of Gottingen University had examined the outside of the strips in 1953, and had managed to decipher some words which seemed to indicate that the scroll recorded the location and amount of the treasure hidden by the Qumran religious community when they abandoned the site.[67] This view was quite different from the one expressed by Dr. F. M. Cross and others, who thought that the document might have been fastened to the wall of the community centre, and had contained either the rules of the lay brotherhood or some other official information.[68]

Metallurgical tests were carried out at Johns Hopkins University with the aim of reconverting the oxide into flexible copper, but without success. Similar tests in England also failed, and it was decided to cut the rolls into strips. Mr. G. L. Harding had the documents transported to England in 1955 and 1956, and commissioned Professor H. W. Baker of the Manchester College of Technology to undertake the task.[69] When facsimiles and photographs had been made of the text, the rolls were returned to Amman in Jordan in April 1956.

When the contents of the manuscripts were deciphered, the surmise of Professor Kuhn proved to be correct, for so far from the rolls comprising a list of community regulations, they catalogued about sixty treasure caches and described their locations in various parts of ancient Judaea. Unfortunately it is virtually impossible to identify the sites, especially those associated with the precincts of the Temple in Jerusalem. The following citations will indicate the nature of the directions given in the scroll:

(3)   In the large cistern which is in the court of the Peristyle ; in a recess at the bottom of it, hidden in a hole opposite the upper opening: nine hundred talents (I : 6-8).

(11) In the cistern which is below the rampart, on the east side, in a place hollowed out of the rock : six hundred bars of silver (II : 10-12).

(52) Close by, below the southern corner of the portico, at Zadok's tomb, underneath the pilaster in the exedra: a vessel of incense in pine wood and a vessel of incense in cassia wood (XI : 1-4).[70]

From these descriptions it will be apparent that the compiler of the document classified the cache in terms of general and specific locality, the depth of the hoard in cubits, and the amount or nature of the treasure. An estimate of the itemised valuables amounted to some six thousand talents, or about two hundred tons of gold and silver. It seems somewhat incongruous to associate this fabulous hoard of wealth with a religious community which had poverty and communal living as two of its regulating factors. One explanation of this situation has been that the copper document from 3Q is merely a collection of ancient folklore dealing with the location of treasures allegedly lost by the ancient Israelites. However, this view scarcely takes adequate cognisance of the fact that the lettering had been punched out hurriedly,[71] and that the finished scrolls were hastily rolled up and concealed by unskilled persons, indicating that the document was probably compiled in a period of emergency, perhaps c. A.D. 68. Whatever the purely historical value of the treasure catalogue, the text itself is of great interest because it was written in the first century A.D. in a colloquial dialect rather than in classical or Biblical Hebrew. Until recently the only literary representatives of this dialect were certain Jewish religious writings of which the Mishnah was the oldest, but these are now antedated considerably by the Qumran copper scrolls.

An abundance of fragments came rather unexpectedly into the hands of clandestine Bedouin excavators in August 1952, and were widely disseminated before news of the discovery leaked out. The Jordanian Department of Antiquities halted the illegal Bedouin activities as soon as possible, and undertook an excavation of the site in September 1952.[72] The cave in question (4Q) was located in the marly terrace of the community centre and about a stone's throw from the ruin itself. In answer to an appeal, learned institutions the world over made contributions, thus enabling the precious fragments to be bought back from the Bedouin. These, along with the manuscript scraps found by the archaeologists, showed that the site had probably housed well over three hundred books at one period, about one third of which had comprised Biblical writings. All these documents had survived in the form of many thousands of fragments, some of which have now been published.[73]

Apart from the Book of Esther, every other canonical Old Testament work seems to have been represented, with several of them occurring a number of times. Of the historical writings, Judges, Samuel and Kings were found in fragmentary form.[74] Numerous portions of Isaiah, the Psalms, the Pentateuch and the Minor prophets have been identified to the present, along with such extra-Biblical writings as the *Book of Enoch*, the *Testament of Levi*, the *Book of Tobit*, the *Rule of the Community* and the *Damascus Document* (CDC), all in fragmentary condition. Biblical commentaries, liturgical writings, apocalyptic and pseudo-historical texts were also included in the great mass of manuscript scraps from 4Q.

Whilst this site was being excavated a further cave (5Q) was discovered by the archaeologists, Undisturbed by marauding Bedouin, it was found to contain a group of fragments which were almost completely decomposed. After a preliminary examination late in 1953, certain portions of Deuteronomy 7–9 were identified, along with a fragment of 1 Kings and the Book of Lamentations.

An eschatological work written in Aramaic and entitled the *Description of the New Jerusalem* was also present in the form of small decomposed scraps, and was similar in nature to other portions of the same work discovered elsewhere in the Qumran caves.[75]

A sixth cave (6Q) was discovered by Bedouin near the head of the Wadi, containing several hundred leather and papyrus fragments. The Biblical texts included small sections of Genesis and Leviticus, written in palaeo-Hebrew script, parts of the Books of Kings, and five fragments of Daniel. Non-Biblical books were represented by a passage from CDC, several apocalyptic writings, one of which was related to 1 *Enoch*, and a number of Aramaic compositions.

Of five caches subsequently discovered in the Qumran area, the latest (11Q), found early in 1956, yielded up several scrolls in an excellent state of preservation. The Book of Psalms in a somewhat damaged condition was one of these, whilst fragments of Daniel from other Qumran caves were unexpectedly supplemented by the recovery of two manuscripts of Daniel in good condition. The presence of an Aramaic Targum of the Book of Job in a fragmentary state was of particular interest in view of the fact that the Talmudic *Tractate* Shabbath[76] recorded the existence of such a document in the first century of the Christian era. According to this tradition, the learned Gamaliel had ordered the work to be incorporated into the structure of the Second Temple when it was being enlarged under Herod.[77]

The literary fragments discovered in the Murabba'at caves from the early months of 1952 were of quite a different order from the Qumran manuscripts. Coming almost entirely from the second cave (2Mu), they presented considerable difficulties in the matter of identification since the papyrus and leather had for the most part been reduced to tatters by the activities of rodents and birds. When identified they were seen to be second century A.D. documents written in Greek, Hebrew and Aramaic. Perhaps the most important single manuscript from this site was a papyrus palimpsest inscribed in archaic Hebrew writing which appears to antedate the sixth century B.C. script of the Lachish ostraca, and which Milik

assigned to the eighth century B.C.   The superimposed text apparently
comprised an index of names, numbers and some other signs, whilst
the original writing which had been quite well erased included a
greeting of the kind which might have occurred in a letter.   A
document of such antiquity is a fabulous and totally unexpected
discovery for a country such as Palestine, where manuscripts seldom
survive even when physical conditions are comparatively favourable.

Fragments of the Pentateuch and the Book of Isaiah, all of which
were dated in the second century A.D., formed part of the cache in
2Mu, and are of interest because of the minute agreement which
they exhibit with the Masoretic text.   Certain non-Biblical works
written in Greek on papyrus helped to date the mass of fragments.
One such dilapidated manuscript seems to have been a marriage
contract and bears the date of the seventh year of Hadrian, i.e.
A.D. 124.[78]   Further interesting light was thrown upon this period
in the history of Palestine by the recovery of some Hebrew papyri
written by Simon Ben-Kokhba, leader of the ill-fated Second Jewish
Revolt of A.D. 132–5, to his guerilla forces in the Wadi Murabba'at
area.   Ben-Kokhba had revolted against the Romans in A.D. 132,
and was proclaimed by certain groups in Judaea as the long-promised
Messiah.   In particular, Rabbi Aqiba, the foremost religious
authority of the time, saw in Ben-Kokhba the celestial luminary
whose emergence for the deliverance of Israel had been foretold
many centuries earlier by Balaam.[79]   Because of this identification
Simon became known as Simon Ben-Kokhba[80] to some, whilst
those who disputed his claim to Messiahship referred to him scorn-
fully as Simon Ben-Kozeba.[81]   One of the letters written by this
leader may be translated as follows :

" Simon Ben-Kosebah to Yeshua Ben-Galgolah and to the men
of your company ; greetings.   I call heaven to witness against
me that if one of the Galileans whom you have protected creates
any trouble, I will put fetters on your feet as I did to Ben-Aphlul.
Simon Ben-Kosebah . . ." [82]

This letter makes it clear that his proper patronymic was Ben-

Kosebah, and that both designations mentioned above were plays on his name.[83] Other letters of the same period and written in cursive Latin indicated that the stronghold at Murabbaʿat had been occupied subsequently by Roman forces. A variety of Biblical fragments from 2Mu furnished indications of deliberate destruction, but enough had survived to make it clear that manuscripts of Genesis, Exodus, Deuteronomy and Isaiah had formed part of the general cache. A complete phylactery had escaped the damage occasioned by animals and man, and gave indications of being of a later variety than the fragments of the phylacteries recovered from several of the Qumran caves.[84] The fact that the letters from this site were written in Hebrew would indicate that the language was still being employed in the early part of the second century A.D. as a living tongue. This points to definite shortcomings in the commonly-expressed view that Hebrew had become a dead language some centuries earlier.

The manuscript fragments which were excavated by Belgian archaeologists early in 1953 at Khirbet Mird, about three miles north-east of Mar Saba, the ancient Christian monastery near Bethlehem, included Arabic, Syriac, Greek and Christo-Palestinian material. Fragments of Biblical codices were also found at the site, but all of the documents recovered were of later date than those from either the Qumran or Murabbaʿat areas, and have been assigned to the late Byzantine and early Arabic periods. From the same general region, but located at a site as yet improperly determined, were obtained some Nabataean and Jewish contracts written on papyrus. One of these documents bore a date which read, " the third year of the Freedom of Israel ", indicating A.D. 135, the last year of the Second Revolt.

Of far greater value, however, was a fragmentary leather manuscript of the Minor Prophets in Greek, which was published in part by Barthélemy in 1953.[85] Written in a beautiful uncial hand, the text contained parts of Micah, Jonah, Nahum, Habakkuk, Zephaniah and Zechariah, and was dated in the first century of the Christian era. It is of particular importance in that it supports the claim of the Septuagint to be a reliable witness to an early textual tradition, and illumines certain obscure stages in the development of the Septuagint text itself. The leather fragments represent a version which is a revision of the old Septuagint translation, and which is almost certainly the text underlying the versions made by Aquila, Theodotion and Symmachus in the second century A.D.

In his controversy with Trypho the Jew,[86] Justin Martyr castigated the Jews of his day for abandoning the venerable tradition of the Septuagint, and for circulating less reliable Greek translations of Rabbinic origin. He even went so far as to furnish parallel readings from the Septuagint and contemporary recensions in an attempt to demonstrate the inferiority of the latter. As a result of preliminary studies of this newly-discovered text of the Minor Prophets it is apparent that it exhibits remarkable agreement in hundreds of places with the Septuagint version used by Justin Martyr and other Patristic authors in the Early Church. It further supports the view that the Greek Bible passed through a proto-Septuagint stage, beginning in the early third century B.C. in Alexandria, and through successive recensions became the Bible of Hellenic Christianity.[87]

Only a comparatively small number of the fragments recovered from the Qumran caves, the Wadi Murabbaʿat area and Khirbet Mird have been identified and published.[88] The task of cleaning, deciphering and classifying is an onerous one which by its very nature must be slow and tedious. Important new fragments are bound to come to light as fresh boxes of mutilated leather and papyrus scrolls are examined. Already the world of Biblical scholarship has been fully awakened to the far-reaching implications of these documents, and whilst some theories as to the provenance and date of certain Biblical books will be reinforced by these literary discoveries, others will certainly require modification, particularly those which have assigned comparatively late dates to some Old Testament writings. Added to all this is the undoubted fact that still further manuscript discoveries will be forthcoming, either from already familiar sites or from new areas in the vicinity of the Dead Sea, to contribute even more to the fund of knowledge made available so dramatically by the chance explorations of a Bedouin goatherd.

CHAPTER 3

DATING THE MANUSCRIPTS

WHEN the late Professor Sukenik reported enthusiastically that none of the scrolls which were in his possession were to be dated later than A.D. 70, the scholarly world was for the most part either incredulous or frankly curious. If this information was true it meant that the textual evidence for the Hebrew Old Testament had been advanced at least a millennium. The significance of this will be realised when it is remembered that the standard text of the Hebrew Bible depends on comparatively late sources issuing from the eighth and ninth centuries of the Christian era. Scrupulous care had been taken by Jewish scribes in the transmission of the text through the various generations,[1] so that the systematising of first century A.D. manuscript tradition which began with the Masoretes in the seventh century A.D. resulted in a standard Hebrew text.

Of importance as a witness to the nature of the Old Testament text in the pre-Christian period was the Septuagint, the Bible of Greek-speaking Jews and early Christians alike. Traditionally this recension had been made in Alexandria by seventy-two Jewish scholars during the reign of Ptolemy Philadelphus (285–246 B.C.). The Law was the first to be translated into Greek, whilst the remaining books of the Canon were apparently completed at a later time by different and sometimes less capable hands. However, extant manuscripts of the Septuagint antedated the earliest surviving copies of the Masoretic or traditional Hebrew text by at least six centuries. Whilst the Septuagint bore valuable testimony to the character of the Masoretic text, it was at best a recension and as such subject to the limitations which beset all translations of an original work. Comparison of the two texts revealed that, particularly in the historical writings, the Septuagint furnished a better rendering than

49

the Masoretic text, implying that the former drew upon a textual tradition which was different from that of the Masoretes.

To unearth such a divergent tradition in manuscript form had long been the dream of textual scholars. But the possibility appeared remote, for as long as had been known, all old copies of Hebrew manuscripts had been destroyed or otherwise disposed of when new ones had been completed. Scholars had become reconciled to the idea of an immense lapse of time between the period when the latest Hebrew writings were compiled and the date of extant manuscripts. It was with this in view that Sir Frederick Kenyon wrote :

" There is, indeed, no probability that we shall ever find manuscripts of the Hebrew text going back to a period before the formation of the text which we know as Massoretic." [2]

If the Qumran texts were in fact genuine products of the pre-Christian period as their discoverers were proclaiming, they were by far the oldest surviving Hebrew manuscripts, and as such of priceless value for the textual critic.

This was one of the more important points upon which heated discussion raged almost from the time when the announcement concerning the discovery and nature of the Qumran scrolls was promulgated. Many scholars were understandably sceptical as to the claims made for these newly-discovered manuscripts, and in consequence there were few who were prepared to take a definite stand on the provenance and date of the scrolls. The first question to be settled concerned the genuineness of the documents. Quite apart from the well-known reluctance of outstanding individuals in various fields of knowledge to recognise the validity of new discoveries when they are first announced, the unwillingness of many scholars to become involved too deeply in the affair was actually a means of protecting themselves against the possibility of pronouncing forgeries or hoaxes as genuine products.

That such unfortunate events have taken place in the world of scholarship is a matter of historical record. Literary forgers have exercised their gifts for many centuries with not inconsiderable

PLATE 2. Two of the jars in which scrolls were found in the neighbourhood of the Dead Sea in 1947. These two earthenware jars are the only complete ones of their kind in the world.

PLATE I. This is the cave by the Dead Sea in which in the spring of 1947 the Bedouin youngster, Mohammed " the Wolf ", discovered a scroll of Isaiah, such as Jesus must have used when he read from scripture on that Sabbath in the synagogue at Nazareth.

success. When the early date of the Qumran scrolls was suggested, some scholars recalled the many fraudulent works which were foisted upon the unsuspecting public in the nineteenth century.[3] In the Biblical field the most notable archaeological fraud was perpetrated in the eighteen-eighties by a Jerusalem antiquarian named Shapira. This individual had apparently copied out the Book of Deuteronomy on the wide margins of old synagogue scrolls in a script similar to that of the Moabite Stone. Shapira alleged that the work had been compiled about 900 B.C., and managed to impress a number of eminent scholars until the truth of the matter was revealed through the researches of M. Clermont-Ganneau.[4] Thus the scepticism with which the newly-discovered manuscripts were greeted was at once a normal reaction and a very necessary precautionary measure. But when it was announced that the cave from which the scrolls had been originally recovered had been rediscovered and officially excavated by a party of competent archaeologists, the entire matter was placed in a very different perspective. The authenticity of the scrolls themselves was put beyond reasonable doubt, and the next question which arose concerned the date which was to be assigned to them.

The problem of dating resolves itself for practical purposes into four parts. The first will necessarily deal with the date when the literary works were composed ; the second will endeavour to discover when the copies of these documents were made ; the third will be concerned with the dating of the cloth wrappings and the pottery receptacles in which the copied works were concealed as well as with an examination of associated numismatic evidence from Qumran, whilst the fourth will involve a consideration of the actual time when the jars containing the scrolls were deposited in 1Q.

From the information which is available at the present time it is impossible to answer the first of these questions with any degree of accuracy. The nature of transcription amongst the ancient Hebrews was such that one proceeded irretrievably further away from the original autograph with each successive copy, despite the fact that in general the Biblical text was preserved with remarkable accuracy. Thus in the case of the Book of Isaiah, the earliest extant manuscript of this prophecy is the one recovered from 1Q, and at the most it is about six hundred years subsequent to the draft form which Isaiah entrusted to his disciples (cf. Isa. 8 : 16) about 734 B.C. The date of composition of the Book of Isaiah, therefore, would have to be decided on grounds other than those afforded by the discoveries at Qumran, which contribute scarcely anything to already existing knowledge in this respect.

The Habakkuk Commentary, on the other hand, presents a two-fold problem, since the *pesher* is obviously later in date than the prophecy itself. Literary criticism of the Book of Habakkuk had earlier concluded that the prophecy consisted of two distinct parts. Chapters 1 and 2 formed a literary unit, whilst the psalm which comprised chapter 3 was distinct in nature from the material which preceded it, though not necessarily the product of a later or different hand. Internal evidence indicated that the first two chapters of Habakkuk were composed *c.* 600 B.C. in the southern kingdom, for the prophet was expecting the Chaldean invasion which was to engulf Jerusalem in 597 B.C. The earliest external evidence for the Book of Habakkuk is contained in the preface to the Septuagint legend *Bel and the Dragon* (*c.* 100 B.C.), where the prophecy of " Habakkuk the son of Joshua of the Tribe of Levi " was mentioned.

If the Commentary portions of 1QpHab are to be dated prior to 100 B.C., this then becomes the earliest external evidence for the text of the Book of Habakkuk. However, neither *Bel and the Dragon* nor 1QpHab would in that case do more than affirm that the text of Habakkuk was venerated in the second century B.C., and would again leave the dating of the book itself to internal evidence. As regards establishing a date for the Commentary as such it will also be necessary to rely upon the evidence presented by the text itself unless it is possible to ascertain the particular time when the scroll was deposited in 1Q, which would at least furnish a *terminus ad quem*.

Dating the Commentary in terms of the text of Habakkuk will depend to a considerable extent upon the identification of the Kittim, since the commentator was apparently describing contemporary persons and events. Various views have been expressed by scholars on this matter, so that the Kittim have been identified successively with the Seleucid forces of Antiochus Epiphanes IV (175–164 B.C.),[5] some military power in the period of Alexander Janneus (103–76 B.C.), whether Seleucid[6] or Roman[7] forces, or the military strength of the Roman period in Palestine.[8] The Kittim have also been assigned to the middle of the first century A.D. and interpreted in the light of the First Jewish War (A.D. 66–70),[9] whilst still other writers have regarded the Middle Ages as the true historical setting, with the Crusaders as the Kittim.[10]

The date of composition of 1QS, 1QH and 1QM has met with as wide a range of scholarly opinion as that of the Biblical documents. The Military scroll was assigned to a Maccabean background as early as 1948,[11] whilst the reign of Alexander Janneus,[12] the beginning of the Roman domination of Palestine[13] and the medieval Christian period have also been suggested as the background for the non-Biblical scrolls generally.[14] The application of palaeographic method will help to determine with considerable accuracy the period of time within which the scrolls were actually penned, as distinct from the occasion of original composition. On these grounds there can be little if any doubt that the Qumran manuscripts are considerably older than the Zadokite fragments.

Some conclusions can now be reached concerning the period within which the Qumran scrolls were written. In the case of the Biblical documents it is possible within reasonable limits to arrive at a decision concerning the time of their compilation. To what extent the contents of 1QH had been in circulation prior to the Christian period is difficult to assess,[15] but there seems to be no reason for doubting that the manuscript itself was a copy of an earlier document, and not the original autograph. It is in the nature of the case that greater obstacles are encountered with the non-Biblical books when one endeavours to distinguish between the date of original composition and the time when copies were made.

If the non-Biblical Qumran documents are actually as ancient as the majority of scholars think at the present, it may well be that they were copied at some time during the second century B.C., particularly if a Maccabean background is urged.[16] Transcriptions of the Biblical manuscripts might have proceeded from this period also, or perhaps from an even earlier age. It can be said with reasonable certainty that the scrolls emerged from a broad historical period which commenced c. 250 B.C. and terminated with the abandonment of the Qumran site by the sect in A.D. 68. Burrows has assigned the earliest Biblical fragments to about the third century B.C., and has relegated 1QISa and 1QS to the period of c. 100 B.C. He regards 1QpHab as having been written during the last quarter of the first century B.C.,[17] whilst dating 1QM, 1QH and 1QISb along with the Genesis Apocryphon in the first half of the first century B.C. These dates do not apply to the fragments recovered from the Wadi Murabba'at region, which originated at a rather later date.[18] In view of all the difficulties involved, the opinions of Albright,[19] Trever,[20] Birnbaum[21] and Sukenik[22] as to the date of the scrolls, based primarily on palaeographic evidence, proved to be remarkably accurate when compared with the archaeological findings which came to light subsequently.

When 1Q was excavated, additional material for the dating of the scrolls emerged in the form of ceramic fragments and pieces of cloth, the latter having formed a covering for the manuscripts in the jars. The potsherds fell into two classes, one of which comprised the remains of about fifty jars, their lids and two lamps, which were regarded as Hellenistic and dated accordingly from the first century B.C.[23] However, some uncertainty was felt about the shape of the jars, since Hellenistic parallels were lacking.[24] At that time the Khirbeh had not been excavated, so that there was no means of knowing that it concealed an intact jar of the same shape as those found in fragmentary form in 1Q.[25] The other group of sherds included pieces of two lamps and a pottery vessel of Roman origin, and these were dated from the third century A.D.

The pieces of cloth recovered from 1Q formed a valuable supplement to the ceramic evidence obtained from the same location.

When the material was examined it was seen to be linen of local fabrication. Since flax had been worked in this way in Palestine between the second century B.C. and the second century A.D., it seemed probable that the pieces of cloth had themselves emerged from this general period. Fortunately the resources of modern atomic physics were available to add decisive weight to other considerations of dating.

This procedure consisted in determining by radiological means the time when the flax was manufactured into cloth, an achievement made possible by the discovery that every living organism contains a proportion of radioactive carbon.[26] Whereas ordinary carbon, which is also present in living creatures, is stable and has an atomic weight of 12, radioactive carbon is unstable, is created in the upper atmosphere through the bombardment of nitrogen-14 atoms by cosmic rays, and has an atomic weight of 14. Oxygen then combines with this heavy carbon-14 to form a variety of carbon dioxide, which is then absorbed by all living things in a constant proportion of about one trillionth of a gram of carbon-14 to one gram of carbon-12. The radioactive carbon content begins to decrease progressively when the life of the species terminates, and because, like radium, carbon-14 exhibits a regular rate of degeneration, the time when assimilation of the element ceased can be estimated by measuring the amount of carbon-14 remaining in the specimen. The half-life of a radioactive carbon atom has been found to be 5500 years, so that computation of the age of an organic artefact becomes a matter of reducing the substance to carbon by burning, and then measuring the carbon-14 residue by means of a highly sensitive radiation-counter. There is some margin of error, estimated at between five and ten per cent, and the present range of measurement does not exceed 20,000 years.[27]

From tests on various materials it appears that certain types of organic life lend themselves more readily to this kind of dating than others. The reliability of the radiocarbon method is expected to become even more assured as new processes of computation are developed. Despite the acknowledged margin of error, those tests which used readily-dateable material as controls have demonstrated how remarkably accurately the rate of carbon-14 degeneration can be estimated. Within the last few years, however, a new difficulty has been encountered in the contamination of disinterred artefacts by the radioactive fall-out from nuclear explosions. When such a misfortune has occurred, a widely different reading from what might have been expected is furnished, and the unwary observer may well be completely deceived as to the antiquity of the artefact being tested.

When the decision was made to submit portions of the Qumran textiles to such a test, the computation of age was carried out under the supervision of Professor W. F. Libby of the University of Chicago, who had pioneered the radiocarbon method of dating. In due course he announced that the flax had ceased to ingest carbon-14 in A.D. 33, with a margin of plus or minus two hundred years, thus furnishing an optimum range of 168 B.C. to A.D. 233.[28] The central date obtained by this process pointed still further to the genuineness and antiquity of the Qumran scrolls, and it remained for subsequent archaeological excavations to throw additional light on the question of dating.

When a careful exploration of the Qumran area began in March 1952, a great many pottery sherds were recovered from small storage caves and crevices in the rock-face. The fragments of tall jars with lids were similar to those found in 1Q. The remains of one dozen jars were recovered from 2Q, whilst a lamp, several fragmentary jugs and the remnants of forty pottery jars were taken from 3Q. As more caves were discovered at Qumran it became clear that the pottery relics formed part of one general deposit, the nature of which was convincingly demonstrated by the excavation of the Khirbeh situated on the plateau about a mile south of 1Q. As was noted earlier, the first digging at this site began in 1951, and was extended because of the initial successes which were encountered. Innumerable potsherds were recovered during the process, some of them in a heap of debris just north of the Khirbeh. These fragments were dated from the end of the Hellenistic period, and proved to be of the same type as those recovered from the earliest occupational level of the community.[29]

The second level of habitation exhibited ceramic affinities with the beginning of the Roman period in Palestine. Different parts of the excavation yielded a few potsherds on which Hebrew words had been inscribed, whilst other ostraca bore Greek letters. The third season of work at the site[30] uncovered a pantry in which over a thousand bowls of various shapes and sizes had been stacked along the walls.[31] In one of the rooms of the ruined community centre a cylindrical jar of the type found in 1Q was recovered intact. The ceramic dating thus pointed to sedentary occupation of the site in the Graeco-Roman period, with level I dating from c. 110 B.C. to 31 B.C., and level II coming after a break in occupation and being dated c. A.D. 1–68. This appeared to complete the history of the community, and subsequent habitation of the location occurred for a brief period c. A.D. 132 in the Second Jewish War against Rome.

Approximately two hundred and fifty coins were uncovered from the ruins of the community centre, and whilst a number of them have not been identified accurately, enough is known for a consistent picture of the occupational history of Khirbet Qumran to be ascertained. Other caches of coins brought the total recovered to over seven hundred and fifty. Many of these belonged to the Hasmonean period, and one coin only has been recovered to date from the time of Herod the Great. Others had been issued during the rule of the Roman procurators until the fall of Jerusalem in A.D. 70, whilst about a dozen dated from the period of the Second Jewish Revolt.[32] This numismatic evidence corroborated the findings of ceramic study, and served to relate the occupational activity of the site to the contents of the Qumran caves.

The excavations in the caves of the Wadi Murabba'at region in 1952 revealed levels of human occupation which commenced in the Chalcolithic period (4000–3000 B.C.), and concluded under the Arabs of the fourteenth century A.D. Pottery fragments from all periods of occupation were discovered, with the Roman period being well represented by ostraca similar to those at Qumran. A number of coins were also recovered from the Roman levels, and these dated from the time of Nero (A.D. 54–66) to Hadrian (A.D.117–138), and also included nine from the Second Jewish Revolt.

The texts found in the Murabba'at caves were from the second century A.D. in the main, although one fragmentary palimpsest papyrus may go back as early as 600 B.C. Hebrew, Greek, Aramaic, Latin and Arabic fragments which were found in 1Mu and 3Mu testified to the long occupational history of the site. The texts in Hebrew, Latin and Greek were second century A.D. documents, and this concurred with the data furnished by the numismatic evidence. The manuscripts found at Khirbet Mird included fragments written in Arabic, Syriac and Greek. They emerged from a period which began with the fifth century A.D. and concluded in the eighth century A.D. Thus these documents are considerably later than those from either Qumran or Murabba'at.

The final question which remains to be considered is that involving the date when the jars in which the scrolls had been placed for safe keeping were actually deposited in the Qumran caves. It will be recalled that de Vaux held that the cave had constituted a hiding-place for a valuable library during some period of emergency.[33] But as Driver has pointed out,[34] such occasions were quite numerous in the long and troubled history of Palestine, and in any event the emergency which prompted the depositing of the Qumran scrolls may have been purely local and temporary in nature.

By far the most reliable means of assessing the period of the deposit is to establish a date for the pottery and for the linen cloths in which the rolled manuscripts were originally wrapped. The pottery is by and large characteristic of the Graeco-Roman period, both in appearance and texture. When an intact jar of the Qumran variety was found in the ruined settlement of the community and dated by the presence of a coin of A.D. 10 at the same level, an even more precise estimation of chronology was possible. There can be little doubt that the linen fabric would be manufactured shortly after the flax was cut, and this took place about A.D. 33, if the median dating of the carbon-14 test is to be followed.

On palaeographical grounds it would appear that all copies of the deposited scrolls had been made by A.D. 70 at the latest. Ceramic dating has indicated that the religious community which had produced the scrolls terminated an organised existence in A.D. 68. In consequence it is difficult to avoid the conclusion that the manuscripts had been deposited by that date,[35] and that ceramic, palaeographical and numismatic evidence taken together support the claims of antiquity and authenticity made for the Qumran manuscripts.

CHAPTER 4

THE MANUSCRIPTS AND
THE OLD TESTAMENT

IT will be apparent from what has been said about the nature of the manuscripts discovered at Qumran that the members of the religious community were profound students of the Hebrew sacred writings. They studied the Law and other portions of the Old Testament day and night, whilst their *scriptorium* afforded special facilities for the scribes who were members of the lay brotherhood to copy out the wide range of religious works with which they were concerned. The fragments recovered to date indicate that the Qumran sectaries were familiar with all the books of the Hebrew Canon of scripture with the possible exception of Esther. If in the end this book should prove to have been the only Old Testament work omitted from the Qumran library, it might reflect the feelings which have for long been entertained in other quarters, namely that the Book of Esther was unsuitable for inclusion in the Canon of scripture.[1] On the other hand its omission might not be deliberate, and in any event some fragments of the book may yet be identified. What is clear from the evidence at present available is that the Torah and the prophets claimed great esteem, whilst the Psalms were also widely employed for devotional purposes. Isaiah, the Minor Prophets and the Book of Daniel were accorded especial attention, as may be judged from the frequency with which fragments of these works came to light during the excavations.

To what extent the Qumran sectaries were in accord with the threefold division of the Hebrew Canon into the Law, the Prophets and the Sacred Writings is uncertain. All that can be said at the present is that they appear to have ascribed Divine authority to the Law and the Prophets, though whether they revered all the books in the second division of the Hebrew Canon equally is unknown. There are grounds for thinking that the sectaries had a greater veneration for the oracles of such men as Micah, Nahum and Habakkuk than for the writings of Jeremiah or Ezekiel, since they regarded the former as portraying events which they expected to be fulfilled in their own generation. Again, the Qumran library also included works which have been designated by modern writers as apocryphal or pseudepigraphal, including the *Book of Enoch*, the *Book of Tobit*, the *Testament of Levi* and the *Book of Jubilees*. Whether these works were accorded the same degree of spiritual authority as those occurring in the Hebrew Canon is difficult to judge, but at least it is fairly evident that the sharp distinction between canonical and apocryphal and pseudepigraphal writings familiar to modern scholars did not obtain during the intertestamentary period itself.

Whilst works such as 1QS, 1QH and 1QM were obviously integral to the life and mission of the sect, it is questionable as to whether they were regarded as being of equal inspiration and authority with the writings of the Hebrew Canon, or whether, in fact, they were held to be inspired to any extent at all. The most that can be said is that the Torah and prophecy, particularly that which could be interpreted in apocalyptic terms, were revered as the Word of God, and that due respect was forthcoming for other writings which had an immediate bearing upon the covenantal nature and discipline of the sect.

The contributions made so far by the Qumran manuscripts have been of infinitely greater importance for the text of the Old Testament rather than for the Canon. A vast amount of new material has been made available for the palaeographer as a result of the discoveries near the Dead Sea, whilst the textual critic now possesses manuscripts which, if they are genuine, as the majority of scholars think, have advanced textual sources to an undreamed of extent.

In the first instance it must be stated that the Qumran scrolls have confirmed the consensus of opinion concerning the enormous care taken in the transmission of the Hebrew text. This is not to say, of course, that the manuscripts do not contain mistakes or corrections, for such is by no means the case. In 1QISa, for example, there are numerous errors of the kind which might be expected in the copying of ancient documents, particularly if the manuscript had been written from dictation, as Burrows suggests.[2]   Certain words have either been added or omitted, whilst letters or even words themselves have been transposed.   In a few instances words have been omitted as a result of what scholars have called *homoeoteleuton*, that is to say, the accidental loss of a passage through the confusion of adjacent words which end with the same syllable or letters.[3]   However, the mistakes in transcription were corrected subsequent to the writing of the manuscript, either by the original scribe or by a later corrector. Whilst 1QISa may exhibit a degree of carelessness or lack of skill on the part of the scribe responsible for its production, it does at least lend impressive support to the traditions preserved by the Masoretic text, and demonstrates convincingly that much more respect must be accorded to it in consequence than has been customary amongst Old Testament scholars of late.

Some comment ought to be made at this juncture on the bearing of the Qumran discoveries on the literary criticism of the Old Testament books involved. When the existence of an ancient scroll of the Book of Isaiah was publicised, questions were naturally raised as to the light which it might shed upon the authorship of the book. It was hoped that the manuscript might assist in settling the long-debated question as to the number of " Isaiahs " who were responsible for the production of the book in its final form. When the manuscript was published in facsimile, scholars looked eagerly to see if there was any space between the end of chapter 39 and the beginning of chapter 40, the place where the writings of the " second Isaiah " are commonly alleged to have commenced.

No such obvious line of demarcation was evident in the text, however, for chapter 40 commenced on the bottom line of a column. At the same time it was noticed that a division in the text occurred at the end of chapter 33, where a space of three lines intervened before the commencement of chapter 34. Whilst such considerations might at first sight appear to refute the idea of a change of authorship at the end of chapter 39 and assign it instead to a place some six chapters earlier in the prophecy, as some scholars of a previous generation had suggested,[4] they do not in fact furnish any evidence as to the manner in which the Book of Isaiah assumed its present form. In short, 1QISa has provided no new information which could be used to clarify the problems concerning the authorship of the book, and as a result the issue will have to be decided on the basis of other considerations. The reason for the break in the text at the end of chapter 33 is difficult to explain. It might have resulted from a change of scribe, or from the fact that a different manuscript could have been employed for the second half of the scroll. Whatever the cause, this division has no bearing whatever upon the composition of the book itself.

Nevertheless there are certain theories concerning the dating of sections of Isaiah which have been refuted decisively by the discovery of the Qumran scrolls. Any attempt to assign portions of the prophecy to the Maccabean period[5] must be regarded as untrue to the facts of the historical situation as exemplified by the Isaiah manuscripts. The prophecy itself is without doubt several centuries older than the earliest dateable manuscript fragments or scrolls from Qumran. In any event, it would appear that the Book of Isaiah had assumed its present form not later than the beginning of the second century B.C.[6]

As has already been observed, the presence of two chapters only of the Book of Habakkuk in 1QpHab lent support to the arguments long maintained in some areas of scholarship[7] that the third chapter of the prophecy, consisting of a psalm, was not part of the original oracle. It must be realised, however, that whilst this theory is consistent with the evidence presented by 1QpHab, nothing in the nature of direct proof for this contention can be forthcoming from the Commentary. The fact that the psalm was not included in 1QpHab need not by itself imply that it was unknown to the Qumran covenanters either in association with the prophecy itself or as a separate composition, whether by Habakkuk or by a later hand. What would only be indicated by the contents of 1QpHab is that the psalm which formed part of the Masoretic text of Habakkuk was by its nature unsuitable for inclusion in a commentary which employed the prophetic message of Habakkuk in a specialised apocalyptic manner.

The discovery of portions of Daniel in the Qumran caves has raised once again the question of authorship and date in connection with that book. According to a report by G. E. Wright on three fragments of Daniel recovered from 1Q,[8] two pieces were related palaeographically to 1QISa, whilst the other had affinities with the script of 1QpHab. The text was substantially the same as the Masoretic, with orthographic variations constituting the principal divergences. If the relationship between these fragments and the scrolls of Isaiah and Habakkuk from 1Q is genuine, it will inevitably involve an adjustment of the Maccabean date which has been widely assigned to the final form of Daniel within recent years.[9] It may well be that the Book of Daniel will prove to be considerably older than has been alleged by many modern scholars.

That the Qumran sectaries manifested a great reverence for Scripture is unquestionable. Of considerable interest in this connection is not merely the manner in which they handled and transmitted various current Biblical texts, but the interpretations which they placed upon the different books themselves. Whilst it is difficult to determine the attitude of the community towards non-canonical writings as compared with the books of the Old Testament, it is evident that the latter were considered authoritative in all questions of faith and practice. The members of the Qumran settlement were dedicated to a strict rule of life consonant with the Divine ordinances as revealed in the Law and prophecy.[10] According to 1QS, their aim was to attain to that standard of holiness, justice, equity and mercy which constituted the nature of God as manifested in the ancient Hebrew scriptures.[11]

Continued study of these writings was incumbent upon the sectaries, and because of this, certain portions of the day and night were allotted to the reading or interpretation of the Torah and pro-

phecy.[12] As a result the members of the Qumran community felt
able to ascertain the Divine plan for their lives and for the consum-
mation of the age, an event which they believed would fall within
their own generation. As Brownlee has expressed it, "the sect
had its birth in biblical interpretation ",[13] since God had revealed
the mysteries of prophecy to the Righteous Teacher.[14] Consequently the founder of the Qumran sect was thought to have an
even greater insight than the Biblical prophets into the sequences
which would culminate in the end of the age. Because the community stood in a special relationship to these processes, the members
drew up their own interpretations of Scripture under the guidance
of the Righteous Teacher.

This leader was responsible primarily for the explanation of the
Mosaic Torah and the communication of those prophetic mysteries
revealed directly to him by God. The emphasis upon adherence
to the precepts of the Mosaic covenant[15] may well reflect the conflict
which existed between the sectaries and their politico-religious
opponents the Pharisees and Sadducees. The Pharisees in particular
were at pains to accommodate the strict precepts of the Law to the
less stringent inclinations of the average Jew by means of their oral
traditions, thereby diminishing the severity of the original intent.[16]
For the Qumran sectaries, obedience to the Law not merely included
the external rituals of ceremonial purification but a sincere response
in penitence to the revealed will of God,[17] an attitude which trans-
cended the legalistic pietism of the Pharisees or the wisdom of the
ancient Hebrew sages. This spiritual emphasis was of paramount
importance since the primary reason for the existence of the group
was to prepare through diligent study of the Torah for the coming
of the Lord.[18]

Complete subservience to the Law was the dominant characteristic
of the Qumran community, for this was a preliminary step towards
justification and sanctification.[19] Having bound themselves by a
solemn pledge during the initiation rites to conform to the Mosaic
Torah in all respects,[20] the members of the sect studied and wor-
shipped together in the expectation of witnessing the advent of the

Messianic period.[21] If deliberate violations of the provisions laid down in the Law of Moses were detected, the offending member was to be punished by being banished from the Council of the community, never to return.[22] Whilst there was an undeniable emphasis upon the legal or ritual aspect of life at Qumran, there was an equal stress upon the necessity for more than the mechanical fulfilment of the letter of the Law. The fact is that the legal piety of the sectaries was in effect an assurance that the community as a whole was surrendered to the precepts and the will of God.

The attitude of the Qumran covenanters towards prophecy is amply illustrated by the Commentary upon the Book of Habakkuk. 1QpHab has been regarded as a product of the oral exposition practised by the sectaries.[23] No doubt this would account for the special standpoint from which the Commentary was written, since it dealt primarily with the kind of guidance for contemporary exigencies which the community expected to derive from a study of the oracles of Habakkuk. The words of the prophet were interpreted in the light of the circumstances in which the sectaries found themselves, a procedure which has nothing in common with the canons of modern objective criticism and exegesis of Biblical writings.

As has been mentioned previously, there is not infrequently a difference in form between quotations of the text of Habakkuk and the comments following upon the citation. Consequently in 1 : 11, whereas the Masoretic text read "guilty man whose might is his god", 1QpHab had "and he makes his might his god", indicating the existence of a different textual reading. However, it would appear that the Commentator had the Masoretic tradition in mind, for the ensuing interpretation read "This refers to the rulers of the Kittim, who by the counsel of a guilty house pass un . . .", reflecting the concepts of guilt mentioned in the Masoretic text. Such divergences may have been due to the existence of more than one literary tradition of Habakkuk, or the result of textual alterations in the Commentary subsequent to its compilation.[24]

But whatever the textual basis upon which 1QpHab was composed, the method adopted for interpreting the prophetic oracles was based on a characteristic pattern. A citation of the prophecy was followed by an exposition of varying length in which the commentator furnished what he conceived to be the true implications of the prophetic message. In accordance with all apocalyptic writings, these interpretations were couched in designedly vague phraseology which would become clear when the time came for all those things which had been predicted to be fulfilled.

The concern of the commentator was divided between the faithful community under the Righteous Teacher on the one hand, and the Wicked Priest, his associates and the Kittim on the other. From 1QpHab it is apparent that the Qumran sectaries felt that their eternal destiny was inseparably bound up with fidelity to the person and precepts of the Righteous Teacher.[25] The very fact of his presence and activity implied that the age of the Messiah was at hand. But apparently the Wicked Priest brought him to a sudden end,[26] and in turn was overtaken by Divine retribution. Originally a faithful priest of Israel, he had become corrupted by the material influences with which he was surrounded, so that he accumulated wealth by improper means and persecuted the faithful community.[27]

In company with the " last priests of Jerusalem "[28] he was delivered into the hands of his enemies, presumably the Kittim, whom the covenanters envisaged as the agents of Divine anger in the last days. They were valiant and proud, the unconquerable scourge of nations, who made a practice of venerating their standards and weapons of war. Whilst the commentator likened their violent predatory ways to the Chaldeans of Habakkuk, he was evidently thinking of a military body whose activities exceeded even the atrocities of the ancient Assyrian forces.

The name " Kittim " in Biblical Hebrew generally indicated Cyprus,[29] and in a wider sense was also understood of the eastern Mediterranean region. But in late Jewish authors it was applied cryptically of any victorious empire in any epoch, and this may be implied in 1QM, where the Kittim of Assyria were mentioned.[30] Attempts have been made to identify the Kittim with the Greek forces of the second and first centuries B.C.,[31] by pointing to references in Maccabees and the *Book of Jubilees*.[32]   Although there are many points of contact between the Kittim and the Greeks, there are numerous difficulties attaching to such an identification. Whilst the conquering armies of Alexander the Great did come from a remote maritime country,[33] those of his successors, the Seleucids and Ptolemies, came from Syria and Egypt, not from the " coast- lands of the sea ".   The conquests of Alexander appear to antedate other factors of the situation as presented by 1QpHab, whilst the Seleucid and Ptolemaic forces do not correspond fully to the des- cription of the Kittim in the Commentary. Nor does it appear even probable that the armies of Antiochus Epiphanes were the Kittim, since the acts of violence which the latter perpetrated were directed primarily at the nations, and not against Israel.

A more probable identification of the Kittim is with the forces of Imperial Rome. Allowing for certain characteristically oriental exaggerations in the description of the marauding conquerors as furnished by 1QpHab, the general nature of the Kittim corresponds more nearly to the Romans than to any other military power. Of all the Mediterranean peoples they alone fulfilled most closely the requirements of being a distant maritime people under the command of a " guilty house " (*beth 'ashmah*).[34] The fact that the Com- mentary spoke of the rulers of the Kittim as following upon one another in rapid succession may also be taken as a reference to the rapidity with which Roman commanders in the Near East were replaced in the first century B.C.

Particularly important in any identification of the Roman forces with the Kittim is the statement that the latter sacrificed to their standards and venerated their weapons of war.[35] This form of cult worship seems to have been practised by the Romans,[36] who regarded the " eagles " as sacred objects and offered worship to them accordingly. This custom was followed in the first century B.C., according to Goosens,[37] and was attested independently by Josephus, who described the way in which the Roman legions erected their standards near the Eastern Gate of the Temple precincts and offered sacrifice to them when storming the Temple in A.D. 70.[38]

...the Kittim were in fact the Romans, it would appear that 1QpHab described the period of the Roman occupation of Judaea which culminated in the capture of Jerusalem in 63 B.C. under Pompey. In such an event the " Wicked Priest " may have been Alexander Jannaeus or Aristobulus II, although positive identification is precluded by the present state of the evidence.[39]   The identity of the Righteous Teacher is even more obscure, and at best seems to designate the supreme representative of true priesthood as envisaged by the sectaries, in contrast to the spurious priesthood of the Temple.   In short, the cryptic terminology employed in 1QpHab concerning the Righteous Teacher and his opponent could conceivably refer to a situation existing at any point between the commencement of the Maccabean period and the dynasty of Herod the Great (37–4 B.C.).

The expectation of the Messianic advent loomed large in the thought of the Qumran community, partly because of the personage of the Righteous Teacher, and also because the sectaries were required to observe their rule of life according to the Law of Moses until the advent of a prophet and two Messianic figures who were styled " the anointed ones of Aaron and Israel ".[40]   The designation " Messiah of Aaron and Israel " as a title in the singular also occurred in CDC[41] as contrasted with the Messianic references in *The Testament of the Twelve Patriarchs,*[42] where a Davidic and a superior Levitical Messiah were expected to appear at the end of time.[43]   From 4Q came an important document consisting of a series of Biblical texts which summarised the Messianic concepts of the community.[44] Commencing with the promise to Moses that a prophet would be raised up,[45] it continued with a quotation from the Balaam oracles in which it was prophesied that a star would arise from Jacob,[46] and concluded with the blessing given by Moses to the Levites.[47]

In a manuscript recovered from 1Q and known as the *Rule of the Congregation,*[48] the Messiah of Israel was described as participating in a banquet, apparently in the newly-dawned Messianic age. According to this fragment all those present were assembled in order of seniority, and when the banquet table had been prepared, the priest blessed the bread and wine in the presence of the whole company.

This was followed by a further blessing of the food pronounced by the Messiah, who thus appeared in a subordinate role. It is evident that the priestly Messiah, whom Milik identified with the Messiah of Aaron,[49] and the lay or princely Messiah of the Davidic line were associated in a liturgical pattern which reflected the thought of Ezekiel concerning the relative positions of priests and princes in the ideal theocracy.[50] The apocalyptic nature of such a banquet is clear, and the fact that the ritual could be followed at any time with varying numbers from those laid down seems to imply a definite sense of sacramental communion with the Messianic figures, and an attitude of expectancy or anticipation of the events which would usher in the commencement of the Divine kingdom.

It should be noted in this connection that the Righteous Teacher was never identified with either of the two Messianic figures.[51] If he is to be accorded anything approaching Messianic status it must be in relationship to the function of the new Moses whom God was to raise up. The Righteous Teacher was indeed venerated as a legislator and an interpreter of the Divine nature and will. In addition, unswerving loyalty to his teachings was regarded as a *sine qua non* for final felicity, and therefore, in a general sense the Righteous Teacher could be considered as *Moses redivivus*. In this event, whilst he would be a personage of Messianic proportions, his sufferings and death could have no redemptive or atoning efficacy. Nothing is known about the way in which the Righteous Teacher met his end, and in any case, his passing from the historical scene was to precede by several years the advent of the Messianic era. As such he was a forerunner or precursor of the new age of grace, not the personage who should initiate it.

Whilst there can be no question as to the extent to which Messianic concepts were present in the thinking of the Qumran sectaries, it must also be remembered that they were expected to be realised in a manner which had elements in common with the popular concepts of the Day of the Lord so roundly condemned by prophets such as Amos. According to the sectaries, the Messianic era was to be ushered in by human strength, and after the Kittim of various countries had been eliminated, the triumph of faithful Israel would be complete. The kingdom of heaven which would then follow would be characterised by a theocratic system, with a sacrificial type of worship under the control of an accredited priesthood similar to that which Ezekiel had envisaged. The Qumran sectaries apparently did not think of their kingdom in terms of a new heaven and a new earth, but rather as the outgrowth of human military success under Divine sanction. Like many people in the days of the eighth century B.C. prophets, they seem to have expected that all nations would then flock to Jerusalem to offer their most acceptable tribute in humility and penitence to a people who were serene and condescending in victory.

There does not seem to have been any consciousness of the fact that the community itself might come under judgement in the Messianic age for endeavouring to achieve spiritual ends by largely material means. Neither was there any awareness or expectation of a regeneration of human society as a whole when the Messianic period emerged. Whilst the sectaries placed great value upon the Servant oracles of Isaiah,[52] there is little which would indicate that the stern piety of the Qumran community accommodated itself seriously to the self-sacrificing compassion which caused the Servant to bear the sins of many and to make intercession for the transgressors.

It is apparent that the concept of Messiahship as reflected in the thought and writings of the Qumran sect must be distinguished very carefully from what is understood by the usage of that term against the background of Christian tradition. The community envisaged Messiahship in a special sense which was fostered and characterised to a large extent by the particular nature of the Jewish brotherhood at Qumran. Whilst there are obvious points of contact with early Christianity in this matter, there are equally significant differences, the nature of which must be considered in a subsequent chapter. A more immediate task is that of endeavouring to place the religious community within the general stream of Jewish life in pre-Christian Palestine, in an attempt to discern something more about the nature and thought of the sectaries.

CHAPTER 5

CONTEMPORARY SECTS AND
THE QUMRAN COMMUNITY

ANY attempt to discover the identity of the Jewish religious group which made its headquarters near the Wadi Qumran prior to the Christian era will of necessity require some consideration of sectarian developments in the Judaism of the post-Maccabean period, which was dominated by three important religious groups, the Sadducees, Pharisees and Essenes. Only the briefest mention of the first two will be deemed necessary, since they are already familiar to readers of the New Testament. The Sadducees occupied a position of great prominence in Judaism at the turn of the Christian era, despite the comparative infrequency of their appearance in the pages of the Gospels. The origin of their name has been a matter of conjecture for some time, with certain scholars regarding it as having been derived from Zadok, the high priest in the days of David and Solomon, whilst others took the view that it had been the name of some unidentified leader of the party.

That the descendants of Zadok were to play an important part in the post-exilic priesthood was clearly the expectation of Ezekiel, and it may be that the Sadducees were descended directly from them. At all events they exercised great political influence in the two centuries before Christ, particularly amongst the upper classes. The measure of their penetration into traditional Judaism can be judged from the fact that in New Testament times all the high priests were Sadducees. As a conservative priestly aristocracy they favoured strong government leadership in order to benefit the rich minority of the populace. Their beliefs were based on the Torah alone, and this attitude resulted in a rather materialistic ideology.

72

They denied the existence of angels, demons, and spirits, and rejected any thought of physical resurrection, teaching instead that the soul died with the body. As a religious group they were consistently in the minority, but despite this they continued to exercise an influence out of all proportion to their numbers until they died out after the fall of Jerusalem.

It would appear probable that the Pharisees continued at least to some extent the separatist traditions of the Maccabean Hasidim in their rise to prominence about a century and a half before Christ was born. They styled themselves the "separated ones", and endeavoured to live according to more rigorous laws of ritual and ceremonial purity than the average Jew. Their appeal to the populace was such that they soon gained an unquestioned political ascendancy, so that in the time of Christ they had become a powerful force in Judaism.

They stressed the importance of the Mosaic Torah, but held that it had been reinforced by the traditional interpretations which had grown up around it. By observing this corpus of Law and tradition, and by indulging in works of supererogation such as ceremonial ablutions, almsgiving and fasting, a man could obtain justification with God. Whilst the Pharisees rejected Sadducean materialism, their own views were in turn governed to some extent by materialistic considerations, particularly their doctrine of future life. They believed in the existence of spiritual beings, the resurrection of the body and the immortal nature of the soul, but in a manner which validated the criticism of Christ that their faith lacked depth rather than sincerity.

But the true spiritual successors of the Maccabean religious separatists were not so much the Sadducees or Pharisees as the Essenes.[1] A good deal of information about the history and practices of this sect has been furnished by three authors of the first century A.D. The first of these writers whose work will be cited was Pliny the Elder, who in his *Natural History* described an Essene community located near the Dead Sea :

" On the west side of the Dead Sea, but out of range of the

noxious exhalations of the coast, is the solitary tribe of the Essenes, which is remarkable beyond all the other tribes in the whole world, as it has no women and has renounced all sexual desire, has no money, and has only palm-trees for company. Day by day the throng of refugees is recruited to an equal number by numerous accessions of persons tired of life and driven thither by the waves of fortune to adopt their manners. Thus through thousands of ages (incredible to relate) a race in which no one is born lives on for ever : so prolific for their advantage is other men's weariness of life !

" Lying below the Essenes was formerly the town of Engedi, second only to Jerusalem in the fertility of its land and in its groves of palm-trees, but now like Jerusalem a heap of ashes. Next comes Masada, a fortress on a rock, itself also not far from the Dead Sea. This is the limit of Judaea." [2]

The style of this passage is obviously rhetorical, and contains exaggerated descriptions which not even the familiar *mirabile dictu* can conceal. Nevertheless, the general identification of the locality with a particular religious community can scarcely be denied this description, particularly in relationship to the sites of Engedi and Masada.

Dupont-Sommer[3] has shown that if Engedi is to be understood as lying to the south of Qumran with Masada situated beyond it, Pliny was in fact describing three major sites on the west shore of the Dead Sea from north to south. However, the presence of women in the Qumran community and the various caches of money brought to light by the excavations at the ruined settlement would indicate that Pliny was not furnishing a strictly factual account of the Dead Sea community of his day if that religious group was actually identical with the one whose remains have been discovered so recently.

Turning from a Roman source co the writings of Philo the Alexandrian Jew (*c.* 20 B.C.–A.D. 50), one finds still further information about the Essenes in general. A rather lengthy account of the sect was contained in his work *Quod Omnis Probus Liber Sit*,[4] in which he described some of the characteristic Essene customs :

" Palestinian Syria, too, has not failed to produce high moral excellence. In this country live a considerable part of the very populous nation of the Jews, including as it is said, certain persons, more than four thousand in number, called Essenes. Their name which is, I think, a variation, though the form of the Greek is inexact, of *hosiotes* (holiness), is given them, because they have shown themselves especially devout in the service of God, not by offering sacrifices of animals, but by resolving to sanctify their minds. The first thing about these people is that they live in villages and avoid the cities because of the iniquities which have become inveterate among city dwellers, for they know that their company would have a deadly effect upon their own souls, like a disease brought by a pestilential atmosphere. Some of them labour on the land and others pursue such crafts as co-operate with peace and so benefit themselves and their neighbours. They do not hoard gold and silver or acquire great slices of land because they desire the revenues therefrom, but provide what is needed for the necessary requirements of life. For while they stand almost alone in the whole of mankind in that they have become money-less and landless by deliberate action rather than by lack of good fortune, they are esteemed exceedingly rich, because they judge frugality with contentment to be, as indeed it is, an abundance of wealth. As for darts, javelins, daggers, or the helmet, breast-plate or shield, you could not find a single manufacturer of them, nor, in general, any person making weapons or engines or plying any industry connected with war, nor, indeed, any of the peaceful kind, which easily lapse into vice, for they have not the vaguest idea of commerce either wholesale or retail or marine, but pack the inducements to covetousness off in disgrace. Not a single slave is to be found amongst them, but all are free exchanging services with each other, and they denounce the owners of slaves, not merely for their injustice in outraging the law of equality, but also for their impiety in anulling the statute of Nature, who mother-like has born and reared all men alike, and created them genuine brothers, not in mere name, but in very reality, though this kinship has been put to confusion by the triumph of malignant covetousness, which has wrought estrangement instead of affinity and enmity instead of friendship.   As for philosophy they abandon the logical part to quibbling verbalists as unnecessary for the acquisition of virtue, and the physical to visionary praters as beyond the grasp of human nature, only retaining that part which treats philosophically of the existence of God and the creation of the universe.   But the ethical part they study very industriously, taking for their trainers the laws of their fathers, which could not possibly have been conceived by the human soul without divine inspiration.

" In these they are instructed at all other times, but particularly on the seventh days.   For that day has been set apart to be kept holy and on it they abstain from all other work and proceed to sacred spots which they call synagogues.   There, arranged in rows according to their ages, the younger below the elder, they sit decorously as befits the occasion with attentive ears.   Then one takes the books and reads aloud and another of especial proficiency comes forward and expounds what is not understood. For most of their philosophical study takes the form of allegory, and in this they emulate the tradition of the past.   They are trained in piety, holiness, justice, domestic and civil conduct, knowledge of what is truly good, or evil, or indifferent, and how to choose what they should and avoid the opposite, taking for their defining standards these three, love of God, love of virtue, love of men.   Their love of God they show by a multitude of proofs, by religious purity constant and unbroken throughout their lives, by abstinence from oaths, by veracity, by their belief that the Godhead is the cause of all good things and nothing bad ; their love of virtue, by their freedom from the love of either money or reputation or pleasure, by self-mastery and endurance, again by frugality, simple living, contentment, humility, respect for law, steadiness and all similar qualities ; their love of men by benevolence and sense of equality, and their spirit of fellow-ship, which defies description, though a few words on it will not be out of place. First of all then no one's house is his own in the sense that it is not shared by all, for besides the fact that they dwell together in communities, the door is open to visitors from elsewhere who share their convictions.

" Again they all have a single treasury and common disburse-ments ; their clothes are held in common and also their food through their institution of public meals. In no other community can we find the custom of sharing roof, life and board more firmly established in actual practice. And that is no more than one would expect. For all the wages which they earn in the day's work they do not keep as their private property, but throw them into the common stock and allow the benefit thus accruing to be shared by those who wish to use it. The sick are not neglected because they cannot provide anything, but have the cost of their treatment lying ready in the common stock, so that they can meet expenses out of the greater wealth in full security. To the elder men too is given the respect and care which real children give to their parents, and they receive from countless hands and minds a full and generous maintenance for their latter years." [5]

In a later work, the *Hypothetics*,[6] Philo again drew attention to the manner of life of the Essenes, commenting on the industry and piety of the sect. He mentioned the common ownership of pro-perty and money, and described their insistence upon a rule of celibacy for the members of the group, on the ground that wives and children distracted the community in general from the single-minded pursuit of truth and goodness.[7] According to Philo, the Essenes regarded wives as jealous-minded creatures who could beguile a man effortlessly and subject his will to continual bondage. A wife who was also a mother was a particularly serious menace to communal life, for she would use her offspring as a means of imposing her personality and will upon others in a manner calculated to disrupt the spiritual harmony of the group :

"Their persuasion is not based on birth, for birth is not a descriptive mark of voluntary associations, but on their zeal for virtue and desire to promote brotherly love. . . . None of them allows himself to have any private property, either house or slave or estate or cattle or any of the other things which are amassed and abundantly procured by wealth, but they put everything together into the public stock and enjoy the benefit of them all in common . . . they have various occupations at which they labour with untiring application and never plead cold or heat or any of the violent changes in the atmosphere as an excuse. . . .

"Furthermore they eschew marriage because they clearly discern it to be the sole or the principal danger to the maintenance of the communal life, as well as because they particularly practise continence. For no Essene takes a wife, because a wife is a selfish creature, excessively jealous and an adept at beguiling the morals of her husband and seducing him by her continued impostures . . . For he who is either fast bound in the love lures of his wife or under the stress of nature makes his children his first care, ceases to be the same to others and unconsciously has become a different man and has passed from freedom into slavery." [8]

It should be realised that Philo had a distinctly moralistic and apologetic purpose in mind when he treated of the Essenes. He wrote about them from a sympathetic standpoint, using his own people in an attempt to show that virtue had not disappeared completely from the contemporary scene. Because of the general respect and veneration in which these groups were held, Philo averred that pagan monarchs had felt compelled to bestow approbation and honour upon them.[9]

The second of the Jewish writers who recorded details of the Essene way of life was Flavius Josephus (c. A.D. 37–95 ?). His earliest account of the sect was contained in the second book of his *Wars of the Jews*, which was compiled a few years after the destruction of

Jerusalem in A.D. 70. There are other references to the Essenes scattered throughout his writings, along with a second shorter account of the religious sect in his *Antiquities of the Jews*, which was written about A.D. 90. Like Philo, Josephus wrote from the standpoint of one who was somewhat sympathetic towards Essene ideals, and in consequence he endeavoured to present them in a manner most calculated to appeal to a Gentile audience. According to his own testimony he had been an Essene novice at one period of his adolescence,[10] but to what extent he was actually involved with the sect must remain a matter of conjecture.

In the *Wars of the Jews* he furnished an extended description of the Essenes, of which the following is part :

" For there are three philosophical sects amongst the Jews. The followers of the first of whom are the Pharisees ; of the second, the Sadducees ; and the third sect, who pretend to a severer discipline, are called Essenes. These last are Jews by birth, and seem to have a greater affection for one another than the other sects have.

" These Essenes reject pleasures as an evil, but esteem continence, and the conquest over our passions, to be virtue. They neglect wedlock, but choose out other persons' children while they are pliable, and fit for learning ; and esteem them to be of their kindred, and form them according to their own manners. They do not absolutely deny the fitness of marriage, and the succession of mankind thereby continued ; but they guard against the lascivious behaviour of women, and are persuaded that none of them preserve their fidelity to one man.

" These men are despisers of riches, and so very communicative as raises our admiration. Nor is there any one to be found among them who hath more than another ; for it is a law among them, that those who come to them must let what they have be common to the whole order—insomuch, that among them all there is no appearance of poverty or excess of riches, but every one's possessions are intermingled with every other's possessions . . . They also have stewards appointed to take care of their common affairs, who every one of them have no separate business for any, but what is for the use of them all.

" They have no certain city, but many of them dwell in every city ; and if any of their sect come from other places, what they have lies open for them, just as if it were their own ; and they go into such as they never knew before, as if they had been ever so long acquainted with them . . .

" And as for their piety toward God, it is very extraordinary ; for before sunrising they speak not a word about profane matters, but put up certain prayers which they have received from their forefathers, as if they made a supplication for its rising. After this every one of them are sent away by their curators, to exercise some of those arts wherein they are skilled, in which they labour with great diligence until the fifth hour. After which they assemble themselves together again into one place ; and when they have clothed themselves in white veils, they then bathe their bodies in cold water. And after this purification is over, they every one meet together in an apartment of their own, into which it is not permitted to any of another sect to enter ; while they go, after a pure manner, into the dining-room, as into a certain holy temple, and quietly set themselves down ; upon which the baker lays them loaves in order ; the cook also brings a single plate of one sort of food, and sets it before every one of them ; but a priest says grace before meat ; and it is unlawful for any one to taste of the food before grace be said. The same priest, when he hath dined, says grace again after meat ; and when they begin, and when they end, they praise God, as he that bestows their food upon them ; after which they lay aside their (white) garments, and betake themselves to their labours again till the evening ; then they return home to supper, after the same manner . . . Nor is there ever any clamour or disturbance to pollute their house, but they give everyone leave to speak in their turn . . .

" Only these two things are done among them at every one's own free will, which are, to assist those that want it, and to show mercy . . . They dispense their anger after a just manner, and restrain their passion. They are eminent for fidelity, and are the ministers of peace ; whatsoever they say also is firmer than an oath ; but swearing is avoided by them, and they esteem it worse than perjury . . .

" But now if anyone hath a mind to come over to their sect, he is not immediately admitted, but he is prescribed the same method of living which they use, for a year, while he continues excluded ; and they give him a small hatchet, and the fore-mentioned girdle, and the white garment. And when he hath given evidence, during that time, that he can observe their con-tinence, he approaches nearer to their way of living, and is made a partaker of the waters of purification ; yet is he not even now admitted to live with them ; for after this demonstration of his fortitude, his temper is tried two more years, and if he appear to be worthy, they then admit him into their society. And before he is allowed to touch their common food, he is obliged to take tremendous oaths ; that, in the first place, he will exercise piety toward God ; and then, that he will observe justice toward men . . .

" But for those that are caught in any heinous sins, they cast them out of their society ; and he who is thus separated from them, does often die after a miserable manner ; for as he is bound by the oath he hath taken, and by the customs he hath been engaged in, he is not at liberty to partake of that food that he meets with elsewhere, but is forced to eat grass, and to famish his body with hunger till he perish ; for which reason they receive many of them again when they are at their last gasp, out of com-passion to them . . .

What they most of all honour, after God himself, is the name of their legislator (Moses) ; whom, if anyone blaspheme, he is punished capitally. They also think it a good thing to obey their elders, and the major part. Accordingly, if ten of them be sitting together, no one of them will speak while the other nine are against it. They also avoid spitting in the midst of them, or on the right side. Moreover, they are stricter than any other of the Jews in resting from their labours on the seventh day . . .

" For their doctrine is this : That bodies are corruptible, and that the matter they are made of is not permanent ; but that the souls are immortal, and continue for ever ; and that they come out of the most subtile air, and are united to their bodies as in prisons, into which they are drawn by a certain natural enticement ; but that when they are set free from the bonds of the flesh, they then, as released from a long bondage, rejoice and mount upward . . .

" There are also those among them who undertake to fortell things to come, by reading the holy books, and using several sorts of purifications, and being perpetually conversant in the prophets ; and it is but seldom that they miss in their predictions.

" Moreover, there is another order of Essenes, who agree with the rest as to their way of living, and customs, and laws, but differ from them in the point of marriage, as thinking that by not marrying they cut off the principal part of human life, which is the prospect of succession ; nay rather, that if all men should be of the same opinion, the whole race of mankind would fail. However, they try their spouses for three years ; and if they find that they have their natural purgations thrice, as trials that they are likely to be fruitful, they then actually marry them. But they do not use to accompany with their wives when they are with child, as a demonstration that they do not marry out of regard to pleasure, but for the sake of posterity . . . " [11]

A more concise account of Essene teachings and habits of life was contained in the *Antiquities*, where Josephus recorded that :

" The doctrine of the Essenes is this : That all things are best ascribed to God. They teach the immortality of souls, and esteem that the rewards of righteousness are to be earnestly striven for ; and when they send what they have dedicated to God into the temple, they do not offer sacrifices, because they have more pure lustrations of their own ; on which account they are excluded

PLATE 3. The Isaiah Scroll, open at the passage ch. 38.9–40.28, is about 24 feet long and consists of 17 sheets of leather sewn together. It is about 1,000 years older than the oldest manuscript of Isaiah in Hebrew previously known.

PLATE 4. G. Lankester Harding, British Director of Antiquities of the Hashemite Kingdom of Jordan, sorts fragments of manuscript in the Palestine Archaeological Museum at Jerusalem.

from the common court of the temple, but offer their sacrifices themselves ; yet is their course of life better than that of other men ; and they entirely addict themselves to husbandry. It also deserves our admiration, how much they exceed all other men that addict themselves to virtue, and this in righteousness : and indeed to such a degree, that as it hath never appeared among any other men . . . so hath it endured a long time among them. This is demonstrated by that institution of theirs, which will not suffer any thing to hinder them from having all things in common ; so that a rich man enjoys no more of his own wealth than he who hath nothing at all.

" There are about 4000 men that live in this way, and neither marry wives, nor are desirous to keep servants ; as thinking the latter tempts men to be unjust, and the former gives the handle to domestic quarrels ; but as they live by themselves, they minister one to another. They also appoint certain stewards to receive the incomes of their revenues, and of the fruits of the ground ; such as are good men and priests, who are to get their corn and their food ready for them. They none of them differ from others of the Essenes in their way of living, but do the most resemble those Dacae who are called Polistae (dwellers in cities)." [12]

The evidence of a Christian writer, Hippolytus (A.D. 170–230 ?), may be adduced as a valuable supplement to the testimony of Philo and Josephus. In his treatise, *The Refutation of All Heresies*, he remarked that the Essenes

" practise a more devotional life, being filled with mutual love, and being temperate. And they turn away from every act of inordinate desire, being averse even to hearing of things of the sort. And they renounce matrimony, but they take the boys of others, and thus have an offspring begotten for them. And they lead these adopted children into an observance of their own peculiar customs . . . they do not, however, forbid them to marry, though themselves refraining from matrimony. Women, however, even though they may be disposed to adhere to the same course of life, they do not admit, inasmuch as in no way what-soever have they confidence in women.

" And they despise wealth, and do not turn away from sharing their goods with those that are destitute . . . a regulation with them is, that an individual coming forward to join the sect must sell his possessions, and present the price of them to the community. And on receiving the money, the head of the order distributes it to all according to their necessities . . . And they do not use oil, regarding it as a defilement to be anointed. And there are appointed overseers, who take care of all things that belong to them in common . . .

" And they continue in an orderly manner, and with per-severance pray from early dawn, and they do not speak a word unless they have praised God in a hymn. And in this way they each go forth and engage in whatever employment they please . . .

" And especially they abstain from wrath and anger, and all such passions, inasmuch as they consider these to be treacherous to man. And no one amongst them is in the habit of swearing ; but whatever anyone says, this is regarded as more binding than an oath. If, however, one will swear, he is considered as one unworthy of credence . . .

" But to those who wish to become disciples of the sect, they do not immediately deliver their rules, unless they have previously tried them. Now for the space of a year they set before (*the candidates*) the same food, while the latter continue to live in a different house outside the Essenes' own place of meeting . . . after having furnished evidence as to whether he is able to acquire self-control—but for two years the habit of a person of this description is on trial—and when he has appeared deserving, he is thus reckoned amongst the members of the sect . . ." [13]

Hippolytus then proceeded to describe the nature of the oaths which the initiate was called upon to swear, the different sects into which the Essenes were divided, and the doctrines which they embraced. There are obvious points of dependence upon Josephus, although the text which Hippolytus employed varied on occasions from that used by Josephus. One significant divergence in the content of the description by Hippolytus of Essene religious practices lay in his omission of any reference to the supposed worship of the sun as part of the morning devotions of the sect.[14] Josephus attributed to the Essenes generally the traditional Hellenic belief that the body was the prison of the soul, from which the latter was liberated at death whilst the body itself decayed and perished. Hippolytus, however, stated that the Essenes held to a belief in the resurrection of the body as well as in the immortal nature of the soul, maintaining that both would be reunited on the day of judgement.

In a treatise entitled *On the Contemplative Life*,[15] Philo discussed the beliefs and practises of another religious group which bore a superficial resemblance to the Essenes. This order was known as the Therapeutae, and flourished in Egypt some two centuries before the beginning of the Christian era.[16] Whilst constituting a monastic community the Therapeutae were essentially recluses, who devoted their time to prayer, meditation, and the study of their sacred writings. The only occasions on which they assembled for worship as a religious community were on sabbath days and sacred seasons. Philo commented on their manner of life as follows :

" In each home there is a consecrated room which is called a sanctuary or closet, and closeted in this they are initiated into the mysteries of the sanctified life. They take nothing into it, either drink or food or any other of the things necessary for the needs of the body, but laws and oracles delivered through the mouth of prophets, and psalms and anything else which fosters and perfects knowledge and piety . . .

" Twice every day they pray, at dawn and at eventide ; at sunrise they pray for a fine bright day, fine and bright in the true sense of the heavenly daylight which they pray may fill their minds. At sunset they ask that the soul may be wholly relieved from the press of the senses . . .

"The interval between early morning and evening is spent entirely in spiritual exercise. They read the Holy Scriptures and seek wisdom from their ancestral philosophy by taking it as an allegory . . .

"They have also writings of men of old, the founders of their way of thinking, who left many memorials of the form used in allegorical interpretation and these they take as a kind of archetype and imitate the method in which this principle is carried out. And so they do not confine themselves to contemplation but also compose hymns and psalms to God in all sorts of metres and melodies . . .

"For six days they seek wisdom by themselves in solitude in the closets mentioned above, never passing the outside door of the house or even getting a distant view of it. But every seventh day they meet together as for a general assembly and sit in order according to their age . . .

"Then the senior among them who also has the fullest know-ledge of the doctrines which they profess comes forward and with visage and voice alike quiet and composed gives a well-reasoned and wise discourse . . .

"This common sanctuary in which they meet every seventh day is a double enclosure, one portion set apart for the use of the men, the other for the women. For women too regularly make part of the audience with the same ardour and the same sense of their calling . . .

"They lay self-control to be as it were the foundation of their soul and on it build the other virtues. None of them would put food or drink to his lips before sunset since they hold that philosophy finds its right place in the light, the needs of the body in the darkness, and therefore they assign the day to the one and some small part of the night to the other . . . Therefore they eat enough to keep from hunger and drink enough to keep from thirst but abhor surfeiting as a malignant enemy both to soul and body." [17]

An additional religious group which flourished in this same general

period, and which has striking affinities with the Qumran community, was the ancient sect known as the Covenanters of Damascus.
The existence of this religious order came to light through the
exploration of a synagogue *genizah* in Cairo in 1896. Some of the
manuscripts recovered from the building were published by Solomon
Schechter under the title, "Fragments of a Zadokite Work".[18]
The various portions of this document narrated the fortunes of a
group of priests in Jerusalem who were apparently ousted during
a reform movement. They styled themselves the "Sons of Zadok"
and under the leadership of one known as the "Star"[19] they
migrated to Damascus, where they organised the party of the New
Covenant. This sect assumed the nature of a monastic order in
Judaism, and flourished under the inspiration of a prominent leader
spoken of as the "Righteous Teacher".

Some pieces of manuscript unearthed in 6Q were found to be
equivalent to CDC, V : 18–VI : 2, whilst seven fragmentary manuscripts from 4Q contained portions of Text A of CDC. This
would seem to indicate a close relationship between the sect of CDC
and the religious group which produced the Qumran manuscripts.
Because the religious ideals of CDC are very similar to those expressed in 1QS, many scholars have regarded the two groups as
identical. On this basis it has been suggested that the community
probably lived at Qumran for about seventy-five years prior to
the end of the first occupational period, after which they migrated
to Damascus, possibly under the leadership of the personage who
was styled the "Expounder of the Law".

Questions have been raised concerning the interpretation of
Damascus in this connection as an actual place. Gaster[20] has suggested that Damascus may be symbolic in nature, and linked with
the prophecy in Amos 5 : 27. North[21] held that since Damascus
was included in the Nabataean kingdom after 87 B.C., the movement
was probably from Jerusalem to Judaea, also in Nabataean territory,
after which the Qumran community proper was founded. It is
true that CDC shows the Damascus Covenanters to have been in
close contact with the Temple at Jerusalem. In CDC, IX : 46 and

XIII : 27, the sect maintained that Jerusalem was their holy city and the Temple their sanctuary. Many scholars who also regard the religious group of CDC as Essenes are inclined to think that they returned to Jerusalem at the time when the centre was unoccupied.[22]   However, this view fails to afford a satisfactory answer as to why the community would attempt to reproduce the Qumran pattern of life in Jerusalem, particularly under Herod the Great, and why the group returned to Qumran after his death.

Whatever the nature of the connection between the Qumran sectaries and the religious group of CDC, it is important to realise that even a superficial examination of the language and phraseology found in 1QpHab and 1QS indicates a host of words and expressions which are distinctly reminiscent of CDC. This common literary fund contained such expressions as " those who repent of transgression ", " to turn to the Law of Moses ", " to enter the Covenant ", " to walk uprightly ", " the season of visitation " and many others. Indeed, the nature of the relationship of language and thought forms in these documents is such that the respective sects from which they emerged would seem to have been quite closely related, if not, as many scholars maintain, completely identical.[23]

The following short selections will serve to exemplify the intimate literary relationship which exists between CDC and 1QS :

CDC, III : 1 f. " And to choose what He approveth, and to reject what He hateth ; to walk uprightly in all His ways and not to go about in the thoughts of an evil imagination and (with) eyes (full) of fornication."

1QS, I : 3 f., 6, 8. " And to love all that He chooses, and to hate all that He rejects . . . and to walk no longer in the obstinacy of an evil heart and (with) eyes (full) of fornication . . . and to walk uprightly before Him."

CDC, V : 6. " They who hold fast to Him are for the life of eternity, and all the glory of man is for them . . ."

1QS, III : 1 and IV : 23. " He has not held fast to Him who restores his life . . . and all the glory of man is for them."

CDC, IX : 50 ff.   " But all they who hold fast by these judgements in going out and coming in according to the Law, and
listen to the voice of the Teacher and confess before God (saying), 'We have done wickedly, we and our fathers, because we
have walked contrary to the statutes of the covenant, and true
is thy judgement against us', and (who) lift not the hand
against His holy statutes, His righteous judgement, and the
testimony of His truth, and are chastened by the first judgements
with which the children of the men of the community were
judged : and give ear to the voice of the Unique Teacher of
Righteousness . . . "

1QS, I : 24 ff.   " (Then all) who pass over into the covenant
shall confess after them, saying, 'We have behaved perversely,
we have transgressed, we have sinned, we have done wickedly,
we and our fathers before us,[24] because we have walked contrary
to the truth.   God has been just in executing His judgement
upon us and our fathers . . . ' "

CDC, IX : 10B.   " . . . when the Messiah comes from Aaron
and Israel . . . "

1QS, IX : 11 f.   " Until the advent of a Prophet and the anointed
ones of Aaron and Israel . . . "

The striking similarities which exist between these citations will
naturally raise the question as to which source is the more ancient.
If CDC, IX : 50 ff. and IQS, I : 24 ff. are compared, it will be apparent that the former attests to the existence of a form of confession,
and illustrates it by means of a brief quotation, whereas the latter
furnishes the actual form of the confession itself.   This acknowledge-
ment of sin has much in common with the confessional pattern of
Daniel 10 : 5 seq., and may even go back to the religious traditions
of the Exiles in Babylon.[25]   Two Old Testament passages (Deut.
29 : 19., Ezek. 14 : 3) are cited in another section of 1QS (II : 11 seq.)
which is paralleled by CDC, IX : 33 f., and again the former appears
to be the older source.[26]

Another issue pertaining to the relationship between CDC and

1QS has emerged from the rather cryptic reference in CDC to an unidentified work, the *Book of Hagu*.[27] In CDC, XI : 1 f., it was stated that all the priests and judges of the congregation were to be " learned in the Book of Hagu and in the Ordinances of the Covenant ".[28] The fragments from 1Q which constituted part of the opening columns of 1QS, and which were acquired by the Palestine Archaeological Museum in Jerusalem,[29] commenced with the phrase, " And this is the rule ", stating that the junior members of the sect were to be instructed in the Book of Hagu.[30] This unidentified document may have constituted the bulk of the manual of instruction followed by the community, to which Schechter referred in 1910,[31] and which appears to describe the nature of 1QS accurately.

The question then arises as to the possible connection between 1QS, CDC and the Book of Hagu in the light of the evident abandonment of the Qumran site for about forty years beginning with the reign of Herod the Great (37–4 B.C.). There are several places in CDC where the migration to Damascus, whether an actual or a symbolic designation, and the reorganisation of the community in terms of the New Covenant are mentioned.[32] In view of the presumed relationship between the Qumran community and the sect of CDC, it may be that the migration was in fact undertaken by the Qumran sect somewhat prior to the beginning of the first century A.D. If, as Burrows imagines,[33] this evacuation of the site took place subsequent to the depositing of the scrolls in the Qumran caves, the Book of Hagu may have constituted the New Covenant mentioned in the Habakkuk manuscript (1QpHab, II : 3) in an amended or revised form. Whether in the light of the present evidence it is possible to identify 1QS and the Book of Hagu is somewhat difficult to say. What can be stated, however, is that both CDC and 1QS knew of the Book of Hagu,[34] and it is possible that 1QS incorporated part or even the whole of it. The fact that a fragment of CDC was recovered from 6Q indicates that the document was in existence prior to A.D. 68, when the religious community was dispersed. If, however, the break in sedentary occupation during the reign of Herod the Great did indeed correspond to the migration of the sect to Damascus along the lines indicated in CDC, it would scarcely have been possible for this document to have been compiled much before the beginning of the first century A.D. On these grounds also the tradition represented by CDC appears to be later than that of 1QS.

A comparison of the various literary sources mentioned above reveals both similarities and differences in the nature of the Qumran sect and contemporary religious bodies. According to Charles[35] the sectaries of CDC were not Samaritans because of the value which they assigned to the Prophets and the Sacred Writings, nor were they strictly Essenes because of their emphasis on animal sacrifice (CDC, XIII : 27, XIV : 1). More probably they were related to the Hasidim movement but regarded themselves as the true sons of Zadok (cf. Ezek. 40 : 46 ; 44 : 15 ; 48 : 11). CDC indicates that they exhibited what Charles called a " reformed Sadduceeism " because of their peculiar tenets, which included a belief in immortality (V : 6), the advent of the Messiah (II : 10), the advocating of asceticism (VIII : 12 seq.), the repudiation of the Hellenising priesthood (IX : 19 f.) and the recognition of prophecy and the Hagiographa. The relation of the CDC sectaries to certain aspects of Pharisaism is evident from the fact that the former also acknowledged the existence of heavenly beings (VI : 9, IX : 12), divine predestination (II : 6, 10), and free will (III : 1 f., 7, IV : 2, 10). On the other hand they prohibited divorce (VII : 1 ff.), and held that the Pharisees defiled the Temple through what they regarded as sexual irregularities (cf. VII : 8 f.).

The founder of the Damascus sect (CDC, I : 7) was also known as the Teacher of Righteousness (CDC, VIII : 10, IX : 53) and the Unique Teacher (IX : 29, 39).[36] His principal function was to act as forerunner to the Messiah, so that as a result of his work the people would be prepared for a Messianic reign. The Righteous Teacher was spoken of as a priest in 1QpHab II : 8, to whom God had revealed prophetic secrets (1QpHab, VII : 4 f., cf. Amos 3 : 7). He apparently suffered death at the hands of his enemy the Wicked

Priest (CDC, IX : 29B, 1QpHab, XI : 4 f.), and it may have been subsequent to this that the community left for Damascus, where they entered into the New Covenant. CDC envisaged the destruction of the Wicked Priest and his adherents some forty years after the death of the Righteous Teacher (IX : 39B), an event which would correspond to the Day of Judgement. Immediately following this event the Righteous Teacher was expected to rise from the dead and usher in the Messianic era (VIII: 9 f.). In CDC, XV : 4, the Messiah from Aaron and Israel was regarded as terminating a period of oppression, which might tend to identify the Righteous Teacher and the Messiah. But elsewhere in CDC (IX : 29B, cf. IX : 10B) the Messiah was to return after the death of the Righteous Teacher, implying that two different personages were under consideration.[37]

The Damascus sect was under the control of an administrative official known as a supervisor or *mebaqqer* (CDC, XVI : 1 seq.), who enforced the rules of the community (CDC, X : 10 seq., XV : 7 f.), handled the financial affairs of the members (CDC, XVI : 8, XVIII : 2 ff.), attended to the admission of novices (CDC, XVI : 5 f., XIX : 8 seq.), and acted as pastor and spiritual adviser (CDC, XVI : 1 seq.). In the Qumran community this same official was also prominent, but his duties were confined mainly to supervising the entrance of neophytes into the order (cf. 1QS, VI : 12 ff.). In CDC, celibacy was not required of initiates (IX : 1A, cf. VII : 8 seq.), whilst the regulations governing community property were also less stringent than those at Qumran (cf. CDC, XVIII : 2 seq. and 1QS, VI : 18 ff.). The exclusion of neophytes (1QS, VI : 16 f., 20) from the communal meal of the Qumran fellowship (1QS, VI : 4 ff.) found no parallel in CDC, perhaps because of the fragmentary nature of the document. The Qumran novice in his first year was forbidden to take part in communal ceremonies of purification, but was not required to submit his money or property to the *mebaqqer* (1QS, VI : 13 seq.). At the end of the second year the general membership of the community reviewed the behaviour of the postulant, and if he was deemed suitable he was enrolled as a member of the order (1QS, VI : 22 f.) after an elaborate initiation ceremony (1QS, I : 18 seq.). Each subsequent year the entire community came under spiritual review as a reminder of the ideals for which they stood (1QS, II : 19 seq.). At this time those who had honoured their obligations of membership were rewarded with promotion, whilst the wayward ones were demoted (1QS, V : 20 seq.).

The performance of purifying acts of lustration occupied a large place in the ritual usage of both the Damascene and Qumran sects. In CDC, XII : 1 ff., it was stated that an adequate amount of clean water was to be supplied for purposes of ritual purification. A rock cistern was preferred as a container to any smaller vessél, and the water stored therein was to be free from all forms of contamination. Particular emphasis was placed at Qumran on the spiritual implications of such rites, 1QS, V : 13 f., making it clear that true repentance of the spirit alone determined whether or not a person was cleansed as a result of the lustration. In 1QS, III : 4 seq., it was again emphasised that water alone would not avail for cleansing, which could only be achieved by complete submission of the individual life to the law and will of God.

The routine of the Qumran sect was such that specific parts of the day and night were devoted to meditation and other spiritual exercises (1QS, X : 1 seq.). The ideal of Joshua (1 : 18) and the Psalmist (1 : 2) was translated into a three-shift system which enabled the Torah to be made a matter of constant study day and night (1QS, VI : 6 ff.). Strict observance of sacred festivals was a feature of life at Qumran (1QS, I : 8 seq., III : 9 f.), and this was true of the Damascus sect also (CDC, V : 1 f., VIII : 15, XX : 1). The religious calendar of Qumran was a solar one which consisted of three hundred and sixty-four days divided into four seasons of thirteen weeks each,[38] and was identical with the one described in the *Book of Jubilees* (VI : 23 seq.)[39] and in the *Book of Enoch* (LXXII–LXXXII).[40]

That the Qumran covenanters espoused a dualistic view of the universe[41] is evident from the tenets contained in 1QS (III : 13– IV : 26), where truth and perversion, the spirits of light and darkness, God and evil, are set in an ethical antithesis reminiscent of Zoroastrian religion.[42]   The angel of light and the angel of darkness were depicted as being in constant conflict for the possession of the human soul, a struggle which would only be resolved at the highest level by the final destruction of evil on the Day of Judgement. This theme was emphasised at greater length in 1QM, where the " Children of Light " found themselves in conflict with the " Children of Darkness " in an apocalyptic battle (1QM, I : 1–17), the conduct of which was described in considerable detail (1QM, II : 9–IX : 15). Despite the apparent ethical dualism of Qumran thought, it is clear that humility, truth, justice, righteousness and devotion (1QS, V : 3 f.) were highly prized by the sectaries, and that their theological system attempted to furnish a means of acquiring these virtues.

Some similarities and differences in the organisation of the Therapeutae and the Qumran sect may be noticed at this juncture.   The Therapeutae followed a monastic rule in which prayer and the study of the Scriptures played a prominent part.   They possessed ancient commentaries which followed the allegorical method of interpretation, and which they regarded as normative for their own exegetical exercises.   In view of this fact, the presence of a Commentary on Habakkuk during the first two centuries B.C. at Qumran would seem to be quite consistent with what obtained in this regard amongst certain contemporary religious sects.   It can be noted in passing that the Habakkuk Commentary itself was allusive in character, applying the events mentioned in the prophecy to a quite different historical setting (cf. 1QpHab, XIII : 3 ff.) in a manner which, whilst not being strictly allegorical, is certainly not literal.

The Therapeutae admitted women to their community as did the Qumran sectaries, but carried their ascetic practices to much more extreme lengths.   They exemplified the contemplative life, but did not share their property or belongings as the members of the Qumran community did.   The Therapeutae deliberately renounced all claims to property prior to embracing the ascetic life, holding that thereby they would be free to aspire to the mystical vision of the one God.   The members of the Qumran community, whilst being consistently occupied in the pursuit of spiritual goals, differed somewhat in their theological emphasis in that they regarded themselves as children of the New Covenant, living in the final age of human history, and under a spiritual obligation to prepare the way of the Lord.

Striking points of contact can be seen between the community organisation of the Qumran sect and that of the Essenes. The latter followed a monastic pattern in which goods and property were held in common under the supervision of a Curator.[43] This was similar to the arrangement common to the Damascus sectaries (CDC, XV : 4) and the Qumran community (1QS, VI : 12). According to Pliny, the Essenes practised strict celibacy, although Josephus noted that one of their groups sanctioned marriage. The Essenes were industrious by nature, and preferred living in small villages rather than in towns or cities. After their prayers at sunrise they worked at various agricultural tasks or industrial crafts until the fifth hour. When the noon communal meal was finished, they again engaged in their labours until the evening meal.[44] At Qumran a quasi-sacramental character was assigned to the communal meal by the fact that the presiding priest blessed the bread and wine (1QS, VI : 4 ff.). However, in other respects the description of Essene practices which Josephus furnished gave considerably greater detail, and mentioned customs not found in the Qumran literature.

The procedure to be followed by Essene neophytes (*WJ*, II, 8, 7) was very similar to that at Qumran (1QS, V : 1–VI : 23), though there were notable differences. The Essene novitiate lasted for three years whilst that at Qumran probably did not exceed three years. In both instances there was a pre-novitiate stage of one year, during which the purity of life of the novice was under observation. For the Essene this period also determined whether or not he could endure the rigours of the community life, whereas the Qumran novice was committed in this interval to a course of legal study. A further difference consisted in the fact that the Essene neophyte concluded his novitiate with the swearing of an oath, whereas his Qumran counterpart took his oath at the commencement of his pre-novitiate period. In addition, the Qumran initiate was admitted to the communal meal after the satisfactory completion of two years of probation, whereas the Essene novice had to serve for three years and then be admitted to full membership before partaking of the " common food ".[45]

Josephus described the oaths which the Essene initiate swore as " tremendous ", and it is probable that he was thinking not so much of the content of the oaths themselves as the penalties which would be incurred if the oaths were violated. Death by starvation would probably be the fate of anyone who was banished from the order, since the vows which were entered into forbad the eating of common, and therefore defiled, food, a custom which may have obtained at Qumran also.[46] In general the oaths bound the Essene neophyte to refrain from wilful wrongdoing (cf. 1QS, X : 17 f.), to hate the evil and love the good (cf. 1QS, I : 9 f., IX : 21 f.), to practise truth, righteousness and honesty (cf. 1QS, V : 1 seq., VII : 6), and to uphold the monastic tradition of the sect (cf. 1QS, V : 8 seq., IX : 16 seq., CDC, XIX : 10).

The general decorum of the Essenes commended itself to both Philo and Josephus, who noted the procedure of ranking according to seniority which characterised their assemblies (cf. 1QS, VI : 8 ff., 22; VII : 20). The conduct of Essene meetings was a solemn and dignified affair, with a strict order governing those who were to speak (cf. 1QS, VI : 10).[47] When one person had read from their sacred book, another would stand up and expound any obscure sections in what had been read (cf. 1QS, VII : 1 ; VI : 6). Such indecorous public behaviour as spitting in the midst of the assembly was prohibited, and this obtained amongst the Qumran sectaries also (1QS, VII : 13).

Sabbath observance was a matter of great importance to the Essenes.[48] All forms of work were eschewed, including the preparation of food. In this respect they shared the practices of the Damascene sectaries, who themselves held strictly to the observance of the sabbath (CDC, XIII : 1 seq.). It is interesting to note in this connection that no specific instructions relating to the honouring of the sabbath are to be found in 1QS, although it may well be that the undertaking which the Qumran initiate gave to honour the principles of the Covenant would automatically cover such things as the due observance of the sabbath and holy seasons. This, however, is not the only deviation from contemporary monastic custom, since the Qumran literature has nothing to say about the wearing of white garments or the disposal of excrement (cf. Deut. 33 : 12 ff.) in the manner of the Essenes.

It will be apparent from the foregoing comparisons that there were wide areas of agreement between the Qumran and Damascene sectaries and the Essenes. In view of the evidence presented by Josephus, it is important to notice that the term " Essene " was not infrequently employed with considerable elasticity, so that sects which were totally opposed on the question of celibacy could still be subsumed under the larger designation. But despite similarities in many matters there are important differences between the various sects. Neither the Damascus nor the Qumran covenanters distrusted women, unlike the majority of the Essenes,[49] but were in accord with the Essene minority group which sanctioned marriage.[50] Whereas the Damascene community indulged in animal sacrifices (CDC, XIII : 27 ; XIV : 1), the Essenes did not, but if Philo is to be believed they tended to spiritualise the entire sacrificial system.[51] There were no instructions in the Qumran Sectarian Document regarding sacrifices, and it may well be that their primary concern was with the spiritual offering of the whole personality to God (1QS, IX : 3 ff.).

A further divergence between Essene and Qumran customs can be seen in the matter of fighting and warfare in general. Philo made it clear that the Essenes were pacifists by nature, whereas the Military scroll from Qumran envisaged earthly armies engaging in physical combat, even if the document is to be interpreted eschatologically. The realistic delineation of battle orders and military formations in 1QM seems to reflect something of contemporary practices in the field, and certainly indicates that the Qumran monastics were anything but pacifists in character.

When all similarities and differences have been compared and assessed, the question still remains as to the time when the Qumran community took its rise. If the historical background of the Military scroll and the Habakkuk Commentary reflect Maccabean times and refer to the reign of Antiochus Epiphanes,[52] the sect may have arisen as a reaction against a Hellenising trend in Judaea prior to the time of Antiochus.[53] Under such conditions the Kittim of the Habakkuk Commentary would be identifiable with the Seleucid forces, the Wicked Priest with either Jason, Menelaus or Alcimus, and the Righteous Teacher with the high priest Onias III. If, however, the historical background of 1QM and 1QpHab corresponds to the period of Alexander Janneus (103–76 B.C.),[54] the Kittim might be Seleucid or Roman forces, and the persecuted sect a refractory Pharisee or Essene group.

Some writers[55] have seen the origin of the Qumran scrolls against the background of the early Roman period in Palestine (c. 63 B.C.), with Aristobulus II and Hyrcanus II as the Wicked Priests persecuting Essene communities. Under these conditions the Kittim would be Roman legions, and the Righteous Teacher perhaps Onias the Miracle Worker.[56] Brownlee[57] suggested that when the Habakkuk Commentary was speaking of the Righteous Teacher it was actually referring to the different high priests who exercised authority from the reign of John Hyrcanus (134–104 B.C.) to that of Hyrcanus II (63–40 B.C.), with the Essenes as the persecuted religious community.

In the light of these considerations it would appear that a *terminus a quo* for the origin of the Qumran fellowship can be established at the latest in the reign of Antiochus Epiphanes IV, and perhaps even earlier.[58] A number of writers have regarded the Qumran sect as an earlier stage of Essene development than that reported by Philo and Josephus,[59] bearing in mind the fact that the latter spoke of the Essenes as having been in existence in the middle of the second century B.C.[60] Whilst similarities to general Essene practices are evident from the Qumran writings, the divergences must not be overlooked. These would argue against a complete identification of the Essenes and the Qumran sect,[61] and if the latter are to be designated at all as Essenes, even in a broad sense,[62] they probably would belong more properly to the exceptional group of Essenes who entertained matrimony.[63]

Dupont-Sommer followed Josephus[64] in adopting the theory of a Pythagorean influence on the Qumran community,[65] whilst Vermès[66] saw three stages in the development of the sect, beginning with a division in the corpus of the Jewish priesthood, continuing in the Qumran stage which was marked by a distinct separation from Judaism, and concluding with the Essenism of Philo and Josephus as found in the middle of the first century A.D. From another standpoint Rabin[67] placed the rise of the Qumran community within the first century A.D. at the point where Pharisaism was succeeded by Rabbinic Judaism, maintaining that the sect was continuing the *haburah* or community organisation begun in the first century B.C. The Qumran brotherhood, according to Rabin, was struggling to maintain traditional Pharisaism against the developing ideology of Rabbinic Judaism. As such they were basically Pharisaic in their approach to doctrine and life, and not Essene.[68]

The nature of the connection between the Damascene Covenanters and the Qumran community has raised the further question as to how far both these groups were related to the Karaites. The latter were also Jewish sectaries, who arose in the eighth century A.D. They rejected the Rabbinical traditions of the Talmud and based their beliefs on the text of the Hebrew Bible itself. Their teachings resembled those contained in CDC,[69] and may have influenced the writings of Kirkisani, a tenth century A.D. Karaite scholar, who appears to have drawn upon some such source as CDC.[70] In particular, his description of the Zadokite calendar shows that it was identical with that contained in the *Book of Jubilees*, which as has already been noted was also the calendar of CDC and the Qumran brotherhood.

Kirkisani also spoke of a cave-sect known to him as the Magharians, a name derived from the Arabic *maghar*, meaning " cave ".[71] He placed them chronologically after the Sadducees and prior to the Christians, but did not give their name. The fact that the

Qumran sect flourished at this time, and that their sacred books were located in a cave might indicate some connection between the Magharians and the Qumran fellowship. The cave-sect was also mentioned by two Moslem writers, Al Biruni (A.D. 973–1048) and Shahrastani (A.D. 1071–1153), both of whom apparently depended upon a lost ninth-century literary source.[72] Shahrastani stated that the sect was in existence four hundred years prior to the time of Arius, which would place its origin in the first century B.C., somewhat as Kirkisani had done.

The discovery of a rock-dwelling near Jericho about A.D. 800 which on examination yielded up a number of books was mentioned in a Syriac letter from the Nestorian Patriarch of Seleucia, Timotheus I (726–819) to Sergius the Metropolitan of Elam.[73] The cave referred to could perhaps have been 1Q, and if so it would appear that the cave sectaries of Kirkisani were identical with the Qumran society.[74] On this assumption it is easy to understand why so few scrolls were recovered from 1Q in 1947, since the bulk of them would probably have been removed c. A.D. 800.

The relationship between Karaite doctrine and the contents of CDC has been illuminated further by the discovery of a fragment of CDC in 6Q, as noted earlier. Thus as Rowley has pointed out,[75] the Document of the Damascus Covenanters might well have been recopied and kept in circulation amongst the Karaites, with some copies ultimately finding their way into the Cairo *genizah*.

Certain scholars have seen a connection between the Qumran brotherhood and the sect of Jewish Christians known as the Ebionites. Professor Cullmann has shown that it was certainly possible for the remnants of the Qumran community to have been aligned to the Ebionites after A.D. 68.[76] Dr. J. L. Teicher[77] identified the Covenanters with the Ebionites of the first century A.D., and took the view that the Righteous Teacher was none other than Jesus Christ. However close a correspondence there may be between facets of Ebionite tenets and the thought of the Qumran sectaries, it must be remembered that the latter were essentially Jewish in their outlook. Ebionitism, on the contrary, was essentially Christian despite important deviations from the faith and practice of the primitive Church. For this reason it is difficult to believe that Ebionite practice rested upon a combination of the theoretical outlook of Qumran on the one hand, and primitive Jewish Christianity as evidenced in the New Testament on the other.

The question of the origin and nature of the fellowship at Qumran is clearly one of great complexity, concerning which the present state of the evidence scarcely admits of a final verdict. The general relationship of the Qumran sect to the Essenes is fairly obvious, but caution should be urged in any tendency towards identification on the basis of superficial similarities. It is an axiom of scientific method that differences are even more significant in all questions of comparison than similarities. With this in view it would appear that if the Qumran sectaries are to be considered as Essenes at all, they can only be regarded as such in a very general sense. It may be that the divergences between the religious bodies represented by CDC and 1QS point to the existence of stages of development in the history of one religious sect, but this is a matter for conjecture. The suggestion has also been made in some quarters that the sectaries were in the same general line of tradition as some of the numerous baptist sects which flourished in the Rabbinical period. Again, it is difficult to say to what extent this may be true. In the last analysis it would seem desirable for a final decision on the nature of the brotherhood at Qumran to be delayed for the present, owing to a lack of decisive evidence. However, it is not too much to hope that further information on this matter will be forthcoming in the future as additional texts are translated and studied.

Some attention has already been given to the superficial correspondences between the life and thought of the sectaries and New Testament teaching in general. This matter must be accorded a more complete examination in the following chapter.

CHAPTER 6

THE QUMRAN SECT
AND CHRISTIANITY

THE community of the New Covenant at Qumran constituted a lay fellowship united in a common pursuit of holiness and truth, loyal to the precepts of the Righteous Teacher and conscious of a vocation as heralds of the approaching Messianic era. They called themselves by a number of titles which included " the elect ", " the poor ", " those who choose the way ", and followed a pattern of life which was sacramental in nature. They engaged in ritual ablutions similar to the rites of contemporary baptist sects, and invested their communal meal with an apocalyptic significance which is distinctly reminiscent of the Lord's Supper of early Christianity. Other similarities to New Testament institutions have been shown to exist in the Qumran doctrines of the Messiah, predestination and salvation, whilst parallels in worship and ecclesiastical organisation have also been noted.

This type of coincidence has been taken in certain quarters to imply that Christian institutions and doctrines were anticipated in a great many respects by Essene thought and practice, assuming that the Qumran sectaries were related to the Essenes in some way. Professor Dupont-Sommer in an early work caused a good deal of controversy both in and out of academic circles by his affirmation that Jesus Christ could no longer be regarded as unique in His Messianic functions, but was in many respects merely a reincarnation of the Righteous Teacher, the elect Messiah of God.[1] If Dupont-Sommer was correct in this approach, the very foundations of the Christian faith might well be shaken by the realisation that a hitherto-unknown pre-Christian Jewish religious community had possessed similar beliefs and practices. On such a view Christianity would have to abandon its claim to uniqueness, and admit that in reality its characteristic doctrines, ethical standards, forms of worship and patterns of organisation had been derived from earlier religious practices such as those found amongst the Essenes. Or as Edmund Wilson, who followed Dupont-Sommer to a large extent in his earlier conclusions, has stated the matter, it would actually be advantageous for civilisation to see Christianity as an episode in the larger stream of human history, rather than as dogma and divine revelation.[2]

In any examination of the relationship between the Qumran community and the exponents of New Testament Christianity, a certain measure of initial clarification of the real issues at stake is necessary. A good deal of unfortunate publicity has been given to certain aspects of the situation presented by the Dead Sea scrolls in advance of careful and systematic study of all available manuscript sources. One of the reasons for so many of the initial arguments which arose concerning the dating of the scrolls was simply that the bulk of the manuscript material which had been discovered to date could not, for obvious reasons, be accessible to all interested scholars. As a result, the larger picture was often envisaged in terms of what proved ultimately to be only part of the total evidence, and this created special difficulties for those who were not immediately involved in the discoveries. Whilst at the time of writing there are a number of matters connected with the scrolls upon which definite pronouncements can be made, there are many more topics concerning which a final decision will have to be deferred until all the manuscripts recovered from the region to the west of the Dead Sea have been published and studied carefully by competent scholars. Hypotheses and suggestions advanced on an interim basis will contribute in their own way towards a final elucidation of the various problems presented by the scrolls, but at least some theories will need to be modified or abandoned in the light of new evidence if the best interests of the situation are to be served.

A related problem is that of the manner in which these findings are to be communicated. Scholarly discussion employs its own terminology which, however, invariably needs to be rendered in a rather different idiom when taken out of scholarly circles. For a writer in the course of an erudite discussion to speak of something as " completely revolutionising " existing knowledge about certain matters may be perfectly legitimate and proper. But if that identical phraseology is transplanted to a more popular medium than that of the scholarly journal or textbook, it may well have repercussions which are totally unwarranted by the facts of the case.

What is perhaps unfortunate about the contribution which Mr. Edmund Wilson has made to the discussion of the scrolls is that, despite his obvious literary distinction, he has in effect transposed dramatic statements involving relative historical fact into the realm of absolute theological values. Instead of discussing the way in which the manuscripts illumine the history of the Biblical text he asks in the end whether the text itself will be proved to be true or false. Instead of enquiring as to the broad relationship between the doctrines of the Qumran sectaries and those of the early Christians he demands to know if and to what extent the latter will need to be changed or abandoned. This procedure is particularly distressing when it is realised that such a contribution was based quite confidently on what were at best rather tentative conclusions, which Dupont-Sommer himself modified subsequently. To accept an interim view of an individual scholar as in fact representing the mature judgement of scholarship as a whole is a hazardous undertaking, and in terms of methodology, highly dangerous.

Another misapprehension can easily derive from a casual consideration of the superficial correspondences between Christianity and the Qumran fellowship. This constitutes the logical fallacy known as *post hoc ergo propter hoc*, which assumes that if Jesus and Christianity followed the Righteous Teacher and the Qumran sectaries chronologically, and if similarities between the two can be recognised, then Christianity is thereby explained and can therefore be dismissed. Since Christianity has always made clear the wealth of its Jewish heritage it follows that not all things regarded as distinctively

Christian are necessarily newcomers to the historical scene. To be able to identify antecedents under such conditions would by no means invalidate the distinctiveness and authority of historical Christianity.

With these considerations in mind some attempt can now be made to examine certain of the concepts and practices common to the Qumran sectaries and the early Christian Church. Probably the most important point of contact, and certainly one which has received considerable attention at the hands of scholars, is that of the personage and work of the Messiah. According to 1QS, the sectaries were required to observe their rules for communal living until the advent of a Prophet and the anointed ones of Aaron and Israel.[3] The Messianic *testimonia* recovered from 4Q arranged Old Testament quotations in such a manner as to indicate that the brotherhood expected three distinct figures, a prophet, a priest and a consecrated layman, to emerge at the end of the age. The prophet was the one promised in Deuteronomy (18 : 18 f.) ; the Messiah of Aaron was a priestly figure, whilst the Messiah of Israel, probably to be identified with the Davidic Messiah, was the lay figure who would perhaps lead the armies of the sect in battle against their enemies the " Sons of Darkness ". At all events, the Qumran sect looked for the fulfilment of prophecy concerning the coming Messiah in terms of three separate personalities.

Christian Messianic expectation, on the other hand, interpreted all Old Testament prophecy in this regard in terms of one unique figure who would be prophet, priest and king. The early speeches of Acts alluded to the person of Jesus Christ as the long-promised prophet like unto Moses,[4] whilst John the Baptist, when invited to identify himself with the prophet, explicitly denied that he was fulfilling prophecy in this manner.[5] That this great figure was an important part of Messianic expectation in the time of Christ is clear from the teaching of the Scribes that " Elias must first come ",[6] and in one instance Jesus Himself was identified with the prophetic personage.[7] The Gospel narratives abound with references to the kingly office of Christ the Saviour of men and to the kingdom over which He would rule in eternity.   An entire New Testament book, the Epistle to the Hebrews, dealt in considerable detail with the priestly implications of the work of Christ in the light of the Old Covenant.   In the thought of the primitive Church, therefore, the crucified, risen and ascended Christ fulfilled in His own person all that the Law and the Prophets had spoken concerning the Messiah.

The interpretation which the Qumran covenanters placed upon the Servant Oracles of Isaiah[8] is of importance because it indicates that the Servant was regarded in both a corporate and an individual sense.   From the former standpoint the community itself, under the direction of its council of three priests and twelve laymen[9] embodied the ideal of the Servant, since by their combined witness to the religion of the God of Israel they would ultimately usher in the Messianic age.[10]   Elsewhere in 1QS[11] the community regarded itself as chosen by God to be an eternal covenant, thus paralleling the concept of the Servant as the one by whom God and Israel would enter into eternal union.[12]

As an individual the Servant was identified with the Messiah in a number of instances.   A reference in 1QS[13] to the time when God would purify all the deeds of a man, and refine him more than the sons of men to enable him to impart to the upright the knowledge of the Most High seems to reflect the thought of Isaiah 52 : 14 ff. What appears to be a decided Messianic interpretation of one difficult Servant passage has been observed in 1QISa on 52 : 14. In the A.V. this verse reads :

" As many were astonished at thee ; his visage was so marred more than any man, and his form more than the sons of men."

The 1881 R.V. made little change in the translation of the verse, merely altering the opening phrase to " like as many were astonied at thee ... "   The R.S.V. followed the A.V. initially, gave the archaic form " astonied " its modern spelling and in general preserved the sense of the A.V. translation for the remainder of the verse.   But the Qumran text replaced the word " marred " (*mshht*) by a slightly

different form *mshḥty*, which probably means, " I anointed ". The
verse according to 1QISa would therefore read :

" As many were astonished at you ; so I anointed his appearance
above any man, and his form beyond that of human society."

On this basis it is difficult to resist the conclusion that the sectaries
regarded the Messiah and the Suffering Servant as identical.[14]

Attempts have been made by modern scholars to represent the
Righteous Teacher as the Messiah, and to identify him with Gospel
personages such as John the Baptist[15] or Jesus Christ. In the latter
connection Dupont-Sommer urged in his first work on the scrolls[16]
that Jesus was in effect a reincarnation of the Righteous Teacher, a
standpoint which he modified somewhat subsequently.[17] His argu-
ment that 1QpHab, in referring to the atrocities which overtook the
Wicked Priest, really implied that the Righteous Teacher was the
unfortunate victim,[18] is an unnatural and forced interpretation of
the text as it stands. Allegro, who also took the view that the
Righteous Teacher met a violent end, adduced as further evidence
a fragmentary commentary on Nahum[19] from 4Q. The Teacher
was persecuted by one referred to in this brief text as the *Lion of
Wrath*, whom Allegro identified with Alexander Jannaeus (103–76
B.C.).[20] Taking a reference in the Nahum commentary to hanging
men up alive as an indication of a barbarous act of cruelty perpetrated by Alexander *c.* 88 B.C.,[21] he inferred that the Righteous
Teacher had met his end by crucifixion at this time.[22]

However, there is no actual evidence that such was the case, since
no information has been forthcoming to date as to the manner in
which the Righteous Teacher died. Certainly no soteriological
significance was attached to his death by the community, and there
is little factual ground for the belief that the Teacher would be
resurrected just before the dawn of the Messianic era, to serve as
its true precursor. The Righteous Teacher never claimed to be
the Messiah, and if the reference in his title is to an established function
or office[23] rather than to an historical individual, there is even less

reason for thinking of the Teacher as identifiable with either Jesus or John the Baptist.

However, it is by no means impossible that the latter had some initial contact either with the Qumran sectaries or with a religious group of an analagous character.[24] According to the account in Luke (1 : 5 seq.), John the Baptist was destined to pursue an ascetic life from his earliest days, and as a boy he left his home in the hill-country of Judaea and went into the desert, where he lived " until the day of his showing unto Israel " (Luke 1 : 80). He reappeared as an ascetic prophet who advocated and practised a baptism of repentance (Matt. 3 : 7 seq. ; Luke 3 : 3 seq.) in view of the proximity of the kingdom (Matt. 3 : 3). The message of repentance proclaimed by John had much in common with the general character of the Qumran sectaries, who spoke of themselves as " those who repent of transgression ",[25] and who were living in a " covenant of repentance ".[26] The belief which John advocated that spiritual cleansing consequent upon repentance must be in evidence before baptism was undertaken was also characteristic of the tenets held by the sectaries in this connection.[27]

John regarded himself as a " voice crying in the wilderness " (John 1 : 23 ; cf. Matt. 3 : 3 ; Mark 1 : 3),[28] rather than the Messiah himself, for whereas he baptised with water, the Messiah would baptise with the Holy Spirit (Mark 1 : 8 ; John 1 : 33 ; Acts 1 : 5, 11 : 16),[29] and with fire (Matt. 3 : 11 f. ; Luke 3 : 16).[30] John believed himself to be the forerunner of the Messianic age just as the Qumran sectaries did,[31] and he interpreted his work of preparation in terms of a desert sojourn and a life of asceticism which again had much in common with the ideals of the community.[32]

It has been pointed out that no great distance separated the birthplace of John from the settlement at Qumran, and that the question of his adoption as a child might well be covered by the provisions of 1QSa,[33] which permitted the sect to train children and incorporate them into full membership in adult life. This procedure would not be unusual if the community was Essene in character,[34] and if this was the case its relationship with priestly families[35] might be a further reason for such a step being taken.

But whatever initial contact John may have had with the lay brotherhood at Qumran, he was obviously not a member when he commenced his ministry.[36] He was essentially an individualist whose very appearance reminded his contemporaries strongly of the traditions associated with Elijah. He eschewed social inter-course, preferring to remain in the desert, where he taught his disciples (Mark 2 : 18 ; Luke 5 : 33, 11 : 1) without at the same time organising them into a religious group or sect. The fact that he would not be numbered amongst the " Purity of the Many " because of his association with sinners certainly meant that he could no longer have been a member of the community when he was exercising his prophetic ministry, even if he had been associated with the Qumran sect at an earlier time. Furthermore, there are cogent reasons for the belief that in his baptism of repentance John was adapting whatever prior training he may have received, whether Essene or not, to his own particular purposes. Whilst the Qumran sect laid great emphasis upon ritual ablutions as a consistent element of community life, there is nothing in their literature to suggest that they required their initiates to undergo a baptism of repentance for the forgiveness of sins.

Whereas the Qumran rites had much in common with the ritual lustrations of contemporary Judaism, the baptism which John pro-claimed was in effect a demand for the purification of Israel in pre-paration for the coming of the Anointed One. In such a case it is probable that the act of baptism was a single occurrence in the experience of most of those who submitted to it, as opposed to the frequency of the Qumran washings. A final important difference between John and the sectaries is that although the covenanters had as their avowed purpose the preparation of the way which the Messiah would follow, a task to which they applied themselves vigorously, they were never privileged to recognise the true Messiah nor to have their devotion used as the instrument for His coming. John, on the other hand, though previously uninformed as to the identity of the Messiah (John 1 : 26, 31, 33), was the one appointed by God to initiate the Messianic period through the baptism of Jesus, a procedure which appears to have brought the Messianic consciousness of Christ into clearer focus.

The possibility of a prior association between the Baptist and the Qumran covenanters may perhaps, if demonstrable, account in part for the language and thought-forms of the Fourth Gospel, particularly as far as the opening chapters are concerned. There are many words and phrases common to 1QS and the Fourth Gospel, and this fact has led some scholars to reappraise the old tradition that John the Evangelist had been a disciple of John the Baptist.[37] If the latter had been in touch with the discipline of the sectaries when a boy, he would thereby furnish the link between the covenanters and the particular theological concepts characteristic of the Fourth Gospel.

In the Book of Acts (18 : 24 ff., 19 : 1 seq.), the writer tells of a group of disciples at Ephesus who were conversant with the baptism of John only, and who were subsequently baptised by Paul in the name of Jesus. If the tradition that the Fourth Gospel was written at Ephesus is correct, it would do much to explain the familiarity of the writer with the background of John the Baptist. In any event, the particular interest manifested by the Evangelist in the Judaean ministry of the Baptist is now seen to be valid and proper. The opening chapters of the Fourth Gospel have furnished a well-informed account of the places visited by John during his prophetic ministry, and appear to provide an authentic historical source for the life and work of the Baptist.[38]

The affinities which the tenets of the Qumran covenanters had with the theology of the Fourth Gospel are of considerable note.[39] The concept of the Logos in John 1 : 3 is paralleled by a striking passage in 1QS, XI : 11, which reads :

" By His knowledge everything has come into being, and everything that is He has established by His purpose, and apart from Him nothing is done."

Whilst there is no attempt to equate knowledge and purpose with the Word, the correspondence in other directions is certainly close. The language of 1QS has its parallels in the Johannine writings with references to the " children of light " (12 : 36),[40] the " spirit of truth " and the " spirit of error ",[41] " walking in the light " and "walking in the darkness ",[42] the "light of life ", [43] "works of God ",[44] and other characteristic expressions.

It would appear that the Evangelist drew to some extent upon the religious concepts and terminology which were current at the time, and modified them to suit his own theological purposes. Thus the Fourth Gospel never exhibits the Iranian dualism so characteristic of 1QS,[45] since John stood firmly in the Hebrew tradition which held to a monistic concept of reality whose ultimate principle was transcendently good rather than evil. Again, the divergence of the Johannine spiritual tradition from contemporary forms of Judaism[46] is partly indicated by the manner in which he refuted those who assigned what he considered to be an improper value to ritual, ceremonial, and adherence to the Law as a mechanical means of salvation.

In any consideration of the connection between the Qumran scrolls and the writings of the Early Church, it is undesirable to read into the various documents meanings which are improbable or unwarranted. For example, there is no reason to suppose that when Nicodemus visited Christ and addressed Him as a " teacher come from God " (John 3 : 2), either he or the Evangelist who recorded the incident were identifying Christ with the Righteous Teacher in any way. Similarly it must be borne in mind that there is actually comparatively little in either the literary expressions of the scrolls or those of the Johannine literature that is strictly unique, since both drew to a not inconsiderable extent upon earlier or contemporary religious influences. However, in the light of the evidence presented by the Qumran manuscripts, it must now be recognised that Johannine theology, with its characteristic thesis of the revelation of God in Christ, took its rise within the larger stream of Palestinian Judaism, and not in either the

Philonic dualism of Alexandria[47] or the Gnosticism of the second century A.D.

Some degree of caution must be urged in comparing the Qumran writings with the recorded sayings of Jesus.[48]   That similarities will be found is only to be expected, since Christ accepted the traditions of Old Testament revelation just as the covenanters of the Dead Sea did.   Indeed it is this attitude which makes it possible to discover in Rabbinic literature also a great many significant parallels to the ethical teachings of Jesus.[49]   Nevertheless there are certain interesting points of contact between the Qumran scrolls and the teachings of Jesus Christ.   In Matthew 18 : 15 ff., a three-stage procedure for dealing with a delinquent brother was outlined by Christ.   Firstly the reproof was to be communicated directly to the person involved; then, if ignored, in the presence of witnesses, and finally, if necessary, before the whole church.   In 1QS[50] the sectaries were admonished not to reprove a brother in anger, nor to bring a man before the whole community for judgement prior to reproving him in the presence of witnesses.

Certain eschatological phrases found in the Qumran writings are similar to those used by Christ.   A passage in 1QS[51] speaking of the condition of the righteous at the Last Day, stated that all iniquities would be pardoned so that a man could contemplate the light of life, a dictum which seems to have something in common with John 8 : 12.   The beliefs which the sectaries held concerning the punishment of the wicked and the salvation of the elect in the final assessment of human values paralleled closely the thought of the Evangelists and other New Testament writers on eschatological issues.[52] As has been observed previously, the community attached considerable importance to the Messianic aspects of Old Testament prophecy. Isaiah 52 : 14 was interpreted in such a way as to suggest that the Suffering Servant and the Messiah were identical, whilst a passage in 1QS[53] which spoke of the council of twelve expiating wrongdoing by just deeds and by living the ascetic life appears to be envisaging the community itself as the representative of the Servant ideal.   Elsewhere in 1QS[54] the sectaries regarded themselves as a

Divinely chosen " eternal covenant " which would serve as the link to unite God and His people.[55]

An anticipation of the twelve disciples of Christ may perhaps be seen in the constitution of the community council, which was composed of three priests and twelve laymen.[56] Whilst the functions of the latter were never stated explicitly, they appear to have consisted of executive powers for the control of the religious brotherhood. Any relationship between this arrangement and the organisation of the disciples ought not to be pressed, however, since it is probable that both were preserving the traditional number associated with the ancient tribes of Israel, so that any correspondence would be largely coincidental.[57] More significant for the organisation of the primitive *ecclesia*, with its bishops and presbyters, is the presence at Qumran of overseers or *mebaqqerim*,[58] the exact equivalent of *episkopoi* or bishops, as well as the twelve laymen who assisted the three priests, and who would thus correspond to the presbyters of early Apostolic times.[59] The head of the Qumran settlement was required to be devoted to his charges " as a father loves his offspring ", shepherding them in time of trouble and personal difficulty.[60] It should be noted that the concept of the shepherd as applied to overseers and leaders was already present in the Old Testament,[61] and was given special significance by Christ when He spoke of Himself as the " good shepherd " (John 10 : 14). Furthermore, whereas the Qumran leaders were at best expositors of the Law and instructors in the rites, customs and mysteries of the sect, the disciples after Pentecost were living witnesses to a unique personage, Jesus the Messiah and Son of God, who had by His vicarious death on Calvary brought salvation within the reach of every individual. They were, in the words of St. Paul, ministers of Christ and stewards of the Divine mysteries,[62] testifying to a quality of spiritual life of an intensely personal and sacramental nature for which there are no parallels in the scrolls. It should be noted that the functions of bishops in the Early Church differed widely from those ascribed by 1QS to the *mebaqqerim* of the Qumran sect.

There are obvious points of contact between the manner in which the brotherhood held property and money in common, and the sharing of possessions in the early days of the Christian Church. The concept of fellowship implicit in the term *yahad* is strongly reminiscent of the Christian *koinonia* of New Testament writings.[63] All the Qumran sectaries were required to live together in humility, zeal and love,[64] eating, worshipping and deliberating together.[65] When they entered the community, the members were under an obligation to bring their material wealth as well as their gifts of mind and character,[66] in a fashion similar to that in existence amongst the Essenes[67] and the early Christians. These possessions were placed in the care of the property supervisor,[68] but the deposits of goods made by members of the novitiate were not made available to the community as a whole, presumably to allow for the possibility of a refund should the period of probation be concluded unsatisfactorily.   When the novice was formally admitted to the brotherhood after due completion of his second year, his property was then assigned for communal purposes.[69]

The early Christians were activated in the conduct of their affairs by a spirit of brotherly love much as the sectaries were.   The believers were described in Acts as being " of one heart and soul ",[70] who refused to recognise their personal claims to property, but had all things in common and distributed them according to individual need.[71]   Despite this degree of similarity there are some important differences existing between the practices of the Qumran group and those of the early Christians in this respect.   In the first instance, whereas those who were admitted to the Qumran fellowship appear to have brought only such property and personal belongings which could be moved, the Christians in the early chapters of Acts sold land and houses in order to contribute to the common fund.[72] Secondly those who engaged in this undertaking did so entirely voluntarily,[73] and devoted the proceeds to social work amongst the poor and widows of Jerusalem, whereas the sectaries apparently used their resources to provide for those of the community who were unable to work.[74]   Finally, the motives which governed the disposition of funds at Qumran were in full accord with the exclusive nature of the sect, whereas the early Christians distributed to all as the need arose, thereby exemplifying the poverty, selflessness and generosity of Christ the Messiah.

Archaeological excavations at Qumran have provided ample evidence of the importance which the community attached to ceremonial lustrations. In a country where supplies of water are seldom adequate and sometimes even non-existent, the sectaries made elaborate provision for the lustral rites which were so prominent a part of communal life. This emphasis derived from the belief that the brotherhood exemplified the true or ideal Israel whose sins had been blotted out by complete submission to the ordinances of God. As a result they alone of their contemporaries were able to appreciate the spiritual significance of the baptismal rite. By indulging in such lustrations the sectaries claimed to receive sanctification of the spirit[75] and the power to walk blamelessly in the precepts of the Torah of God. But the very fact that a person participated in ceremonial washings did not of itself produce spiritual purity and moral rectitude. Any thought of an *ex opere operato* efficacy attached to the rite was pointedly refuted by the statement in 1QS that participants would not be cleansed unless and until they had turned away from their wickedness and had taken the oath of allegiance to the community.[76] Because it was the spirit of God who in actuality cleansed a person from sin and iniquity, the sanctifying of the individual would constitute a gradual process, which would be completed by a direct act of Divine grace at the Judgement.[77] Baptism by the Holy Spirit of God was thought by the sectaries to have been bestowed upon the Messiah in order to forestall contamination by evil forces,[78] and also upon His anointed followers,[79] since the Messiah was to " sprinkle many nations ".[80]

There is no indication in the Qumran literature as to the manner in which these purificatory rites were conducted. As long as an adequate amount of water was available, the ablutions could be carried out in proper conformity to the community rule in the absence of specific directions as to the mode which was to be employed. Probably this same degree of freedom also obtained amongst other contemporary baptist sects in Palestine, so that a baptism was equally valid whether it was achieved by means of affusion, immersion or some other method. The principal difference between the Qumran lustrations and Christian baptism resides in the frequency with which the act was undertaken and the peculiarly sacramental character of the Christian rite. Amongst the sectaries ceremonial washings were a common occurrence, and were not restricted to initiation into the community. Whilst they were intended to symbolise the operation of Divine grace in the individual, they did not assume the unique character of the Christian initiatory rite, performed once only in the Name of the Trinity. Nor were the Qumran lustrations intended for any others than the sectaries themselves, so that the thought of baptising every nation in the triune Name was an evangelistic concept completely foreign to the Qumran community.

The second principal rite found amongst the sectaries was the sacred communal meal, described in some detail in 1QS. Provision was made for all to dine together, and after the members were assembled in their appointed order, the priest blessed the bread and wine, after which all partook of the meal.[81] In 1QSa the Messianic nature of the repast was envisaged by including in the assembly the personage of the Anointed One of God, who gave a second blessing to supplement that pronounced by the priest. There are reasons for thinking that the rite may have been drawn up as an anticipation of the Messianic banquet which was expected to take place with the dawning of the new age of grace. Such a feast would be attended by the priestly and Davidic Messiahs, the elders and sages of Israel, and the faithful congregation.

This procedure had much in common with the description furnished by Josephus of the Essene sacramental meal.[82] After bathing in cold water the Essenes put on clean white robes, a custom which may have been borrowed from Egyptian religion, and then took their appointed places in the dining hall. When the food had been placed upon the table it was blessed by a priest and the meal commenced. When all had eaten a concluding grace was pronounced and the community subsequently dispersed. This procedure took place daily at the noon and evening meals, and according to Josephus was the Essene version of the ritual banquet in the Temple.

The Essene and Qumran rites constitute important parallels to the Christian service of the Lord's Supper. The primitive " breaking of bread " [83] which according to the accounts in 1 Corinthians often took the form of a communal meal (*agape*), was presided over by the leader and followed by a celebration of the Holy Communion,[84] in which the bread and wine were blessed by the celebrant. It is evident that both the Qumran and the Christian rites exhibited pronounced Messianic and apocalyptic characteristics, whilst the idea of a Messianic banquet at the end of the age was clearly linked by Christ with the Last Supper when He promised His disciples that they would eat and drink at His table in His coming kingdom.[85]

A curious reflection of the procedural rules contained in 1QS has been seen in the incident which took place immediately after Christ declared that someone would betray Him.[86] In considerable surprise Peter beckoned to the disciple who was " leaning on Jesus' bosom " and asked him to ascertain from Christ the identity of the offender. Now the Qumran sectaries when in session were obliged to follow a set procedure in which the interruption of an address was as much an offence as speaking out of turn.[87] Thus in the light of this practice it would appear that John, who sat next to Jesus, was accorded seniority and was the one to address to Jesus questions asked by inferior members of the group. On this basis it is clear that whatever primacy Peter may be alleged to have exercised subsequently, he did not rank supreme amongst the disciples at this time. Indeed, the question of precedence was evidently a matter of some dispute on this occasion, since the group began to quarrel over seniority.[88] No doubt the disciples thought that the order of seating at the Last Supper would govern their future ranking in the Kingdom of God, a supposition which is quite probable if the disciples were at all influenced by considerations of ranking which were so important to both the Essenes and the Qumran brotherhood.

It is matters such as these that have led some scholars to see the background of the Lord's Supper in the communal rites of some such group as the Qumran sectaries rather than in Passover celebrations.[89] This view ignores the stated fact that Christ was actually celebrating the Passover with His disciples according to the age-old rite,[90] following which He instituted one of the two sacraments which He prescribed for His followers. This communal meal was intended to symbolise the one full, perfect and sufficient sacrifice for human sin, to remind the participants of the claim which the atoning death of Jesus the Messiah had upon their lives, to assure them of continued grace and support as they lived by His power, and to extend to them the blessed hope of His return in glory to bring to an end the affairs of the age. Thus it is important to remember that by celebrating the Passover in the larger form of the Last Supper, Christ the anti-type of the traditional Passover sacrifice was revealing Himself as the promised Lamb of God who should atone for human sin by His death on the Cross.[91]

Whatever functions of government the Qumran sectaries may have ascribed to the Messiah, it is clear from their writings that He was never expected to die for human sin. For the community sin was an individual matter, and not inherited as the result of a pristine declension from grace. Salvation began when the individual attained to a measure of spiritual discernment through the agency of the twin spirits of light and truth. Since there was no concept of universal sin, there was naturally no need for an atonement of the kind achieved by the death of Christ on Calvary.

Again, the concept of the communal meal both at Qumran and amongst the Essene sects was not envisaged against the same background of worship on an assigned day of the week as was the case with the Christian observance of the Lord's Supper. In fact, there is probably more to be said for the correspondence between the Qumran or Essene practices in this respect and those of the *habhuroth* than for early Christian communion ritual. The *habhuroth* consisted of associations of pious Jews who kept aloof from the common man so as to avoid being contaminated through contact with impurity and infidelity. These "companions", as they are sometimes styled, did not live a communal life in the generally accepted sense, and according to the Mishna did not participate in the common ownership of property as at Qumran.[92] The strict rules of purity which the institution enjoined required a "companion" (habher) to be in a state of ceremonial cleanness before partaking of food, and forbad him to eat a meal which had been prepared by one who was not a habher. They assembled for meals which followed the general pattern of the Passover celebration, and were attended by groups of ten.[93] The meals may also have had some connection with the priestly repasts in the Temple, which because of the consecrated nature of the food, proceeding as it did from tithes, offerings and sacrifices, assumed a more religious character than would have been the case otherwise.[94]

Interesting light has been shed by the Qumran texts upon the way in which New Testament writers, when quoting the Old Testament, tended to paraphrase rather than to cite the passage in question exactly. Whilst Old Testament quotations occurring in the New Testament were generally taken from the Septuagint, the Bible of the Early Church, rather than from the Hebrew, the various writers often treated the passages which they were quoting in a rather free fashion which amounted in some cases to an interpretation of the text rather than a direct citation.[95] A familiar example concerning the foretelling of the birth of Christ is to be found in the Gospel of Matthew, where the Evangelist writes :

"And you, Bethlehem, land of Judah, are by no means least amongst the princes of Judah, for from you shall proceed a governor who shall shepherd my people Israel." [96]

The reference was obviously to the prophecy in Micah (5 : 2), where the Masoretic text, with the almost complete support of the Septuagint, states :

"But you, Bethlehem Ephrathah, though of little account amongst the families of Judah, from you shall one proceed unto me that is to be ruler in Israel, whose origin is of old."

Whilst Matthew has followed Micah in recognising the emergence of a notable personage, he has altered the functions of this individual and has also assigned to Bethlehem a prominence not contemplated by the prophet whom he is quoting. Israel was envisaged as a religious community rather than a monarchy, the "families" (*thousands*) became "princes", and the ancient designation Ephrathah was altered to "land of Judah". Thus the Matthean citation, which has no support from any textual tradition, has interpreted the prophetic passage from a special standpoint characteristic of the Evangelist.

An analogous treatment of prophecy can be seen in 1QpHab, I : 13, where the interrogative singular "do you look" of the Masoretic text has been altered to the plural in order that the commentator might inveigh against a perfidious group designated as the "house of Absalom" who evidently stood in much the same relationship to the Righteous Teacher as the Edomites did to the Israelites when the latter were being taken into captivity. Thus in the most succinct Old Testament statement of the issues involved in the problem of evil, the commentator deliberately diverted the attention of the reader to the affairs of the sectaries in their conflict with the Wicked Priest, thereby imposing a special interpretation upon the prophetic utterance which was not in the mind of the original writer.[97]

In the light of the Messianic *testimonia* recovered from 4Q, it seems probable that a collection of "logia" lies behind the Old Testament quotations in Matthew, and perhaps behind the other synoptic Gospels also. There now appears to be no adequate reason to doubt that such groups of material were employed by the early Christian Church for purposes of preaching and teaching. In the case of the First Gospel, the "oracles" (*logia*) which according to Papias were composed by Matthew in the Hebrew language,[98] may have consisted of a series of Old Testament Messianic proof-texts[99] following pre-Masoretic textual traditions.

Some parallels between the Qumran writings and the language of St. Paul and other New Testament writers are worthy of notice. The moral connotation which St. Paul attached to the term

" flesh " [100] is found in the scrolls,[101] whilst there is also a large area of agreement in the concept of " spirit ",[102] despite the absence of parallels to such New Testament phrases as " the spirit of the world " (1 Cor. 2 : 12) or " the spirit of (or from) God " (Rom. 8 : 9 ; 1 John 4 : 2, al.). The sectaries called themselves the " sons of light ", a title which was also employed in the New Testament (Luke 16 : 8 ; John 12 : 36 ; 1 Thess. 5 : 5), and " the men of Divine choosing ",[103] which is reminiscent of " the chosen " or " the called " of Pauline phraseology. A comparison of the list of vices said in 1QS to result from the functioning within the human personality of the spirit of perversity[104] with what St. Paul has to say about the " works of the flesh " [105] indicates that both the sectaries and the Apostle expressed analogous sentiments concerning the operation of unregenerate human nature.

Some similarities to the doctrine of justification by faith, which is so characteristic of Pauline thought,[106] are also to be found in the Qumran scrolls. The hymns of the sectaries frequently reflected the concept that works of righteousness were to be found in God alone,[107] whilst 1QS stated explicitly that justification belonged to God, who dispensed it in accordance with the mercy and righteousness typical of the Divine nature.[108] A personal faith in the Righteous Teacher was also regarded in 1QpHab as a means of salvation from the fate which would overtake those who did not live according to the tenets of the Law.[109] From these occurrences it will be seen that the concept of justification envisaged by the brotherhood at Qumran was essentially that of the Old Testament men of God, and has little relationship to the Pauline doctrine of a living personal union with Christ. Furthermore, the Qumran teaching concerning sanctification was apparently intimately connected with the processes of justification through Divine mercy, whereas in the thought of St. Paul this developing and refining of personal spirituality, whilst naturally dependent upon justification, was the peculiar function of the Holy Spirit.

It is perhaps not without significance that the New Testament book which Luther castigated as " a right strawy gospel " exhibits certain parallels in thought and phraseology to the writings of the sectaries. The Epistle of James may be said to represent the standpoint of those Jews who had been converted to the teachings of Jesus without being unduly influenced by the doctrinal presuppositions of Paulinism. As such these early Christians might be expected to have somewhat more in common with the Qumran fellowship than would have been the case with the Christians of Asia Minor, Greece or Italy. When James spoke of "temptation" or "trial" (1 : 12), he was treating of a theme which was familiar to the Qumran brotherhood,[110] whilst the reward of a "crown of life" for the Christian was paralleled at Qumran by a glorious diadem and a beautiful robe.[111] The enticement of the unwary (1 : 14) found its counterpart in the hymns of the religious sect,[112] which spoke of nets and traps being set for the worldly-minded. In James 4 : 5, the statement concerning the Divine spirit in man "lusting to envy", a quotation which the author attributed to Scripture, may in fact be a reflection of the Qumran writings and not a citation from the Old Testament, in which it does not appear.

The spirit of perversity was spoken of in 1QS as disposed towards greed, pride, untruth, deception and the like,[113] and since according to the sectaries this spirit dwelt in man in company with the spirit of truth, it may be that James was referring to 1QS when he spoke of "the Scripture".[114] Due to the fact that extra-Biblical literature was referred to by Jude (vs. 9, 14 f.),[115] there may be some warrant for James indulging in the same practice, particularly since the two letters are not completely unrelated in standpoint and theology.

The second Epistle of Peter, with its emphasis upon brotherly love, the true way, light in the midst of darkness, true and false teachers and the final destruction of the world by fire, is distinctly reminiscent of the writings in the possession of the lay brotherhood. Consequently it is now no longer necessary to suppose that the Epistle was written about the middle of the second century A.D., as is generally maintained by critical scholars. Nor is there any reason for asserting that it proceeded from any other than a strictly Palestinian Jewish milieu, related closely to the thought of the

Essenes and similar sects which flourished at the beginning of the Christian era.

It will be apparent from the foregoing that while there are obvious similarities between the thought and practice of the Qumran community and that of the early Christians, there are also notable and far-reaching differences. The religious group which made its home to the west of the Dead Sea was essentially Jewish in nature, oriented in terms of Mosaic legalism and controlled by priests. The tenets of the sectaries presupposed an acquaintance with Iranian dualism which represented a marked departure from the monism of traditional Hebrew thought. The brotherhood was exclusive in nature, dedicated to a life of asceticism, and committed to a policy of military activity as one means of achieving the goal of Messianism. By contrast the early Christian Church was fostered by the little band of disciples under the guidance of the Holy Spirit and brought to bear upon the nations of the Mediterranean Sea and beyond. The atoning work of Christ and the teachings which He had promulgated fulfilled the highest expectations of the Law and prophecy, and in transcending them furnished nascent Christianity with its unique message of redemption from sin through repentance and spiritual union with the crucified and risen Lord. The fellowship which characterised early Christianity bore no traces of exclusiveness, for Christ had commanded that the Gospel should be preached to all nations, and His followers were quick to rise to the challenge. The gift of the Holy Spirit at Pentecost completed the revelation of the Trinity in unity, with the result that Old Testament monotheism was replaced by Trinitarianism. In the sphere of practical conduct, the disciples followed the injunction of Christ to love their enemies and exercise Christian charity towards those who persecuted them.

Whilst the writings of the sect exhibited certain points of contact with the documents which proceeded from the Apostolic circle, it is significant that the cardinal Christian doctrines of the incarnate Deity, original sin, redemption through the work of Calvary, and the activity of the Holy Spirit as a normative part of Christian experience are nowhere to be found in the Dead Sea scrolls.

Nevertheless the manuscripts have achieved something more than the incidental illumination of the background of early Christianity in matters of history and thought. They have furnished a convincing picture of the cultural and religious milieu from which John the Baptist and Jesus emerged, and have also provided a clearer insight into the dilemma which confronted contemporary Judaism. Already it is apparent that the relationship between developing Christianity and the current religious bodies of an Essene character is in many respects more intimate and noteworthy than that between Christianity and Rabbinic Judaism. On the other hand, caution must be urged when any attempt is made to estimate the significance of the parallels between Christianity and the teachings of the Qumran sect, particularly if the latter are regarded as Essene in nature.

Quite apart from the doctrinal differences mentioned above, the attitude of Essenism generally towards early Christianity was hostile, as Hegesippus noted in his *Memoirs*.[116] This reaction would be less likely if, as F. M. Cross has maintained, " the Essene documents are documents of this (i.e. Biblical) faith, testimony to that same faith which became Christianity in the fulness of time ".[117] In short, something more than a casual divergence by Christianity from a quasi-Essene background appears to have taken place. As regards the two Christian sacraments, there is no evidence that baptism was ever borrowed directly from the Essenes or related groups, whilst the institution of the Lord's Supper was bound up intimately with the ancient Passover ritual and invested with a unique eschatological significance completely foreign to the thought of the sectaries at Qumran.

What is evident from a study of the scrolls is that the historical relationship between Judaism and nascent Christianity must continue to receive consistent emphasis. At the same time the fundamental theological differences between those under Law and those under Grace have been brought into an even sharper focus. The Qumran documents have provided a fresh stimulus for the study of the characteristic theological doctrines of Christianity against a more assured historical background. Whilst incidental light has been shed upon many New Testament passages, no literary source discovered to the present has altered in any way the unique elements of Christianity, nor have they made necessary any changes in traditional Christian doctrine.

The coming years will undoubtedly see a continuation of the studies so far elicited by the discovery of the scrolls. In a short chapter such as this it is impossible to attempt more than a rather brief consideration of certain aspects of recent studies. There can, however, be no doubt that the Qumran manuscripts have provided a fertile field for scholarly activity, the effects of which will become more apparent as time goes on. Some of the conclusions arrived at in the present survey of the Qumran material will of necessity be rather tentative in nature. On these no final pronouncements can be made until all the documents which were found have been published and studied by competent scholars. The initial furore over such matters as the interpretation of certain passages in the scrolls and the date of the manuscripts generally has given place to a deeper and fuller consideration of the historical background from which the scrolls emerged, and subsequent decades can be expected to produce careful objective studies designed to explore as fully as possible the significance of the Dead Sea scrolls for history and faith.

NOTES TO CHAPTERS

CHAPTER ONE

1. A more accurate designation of the earliest documents discovered is the Qumran scrolls, since the general area lying to the west of the Dead Sea contains three distinct localities from which manuscripts to be considered in the present work were recovered. The principal sites are as follows : at or near the Wadi Qumran, north-west of the Dead Sea (1947-55) ; the Wadi Murabba'at, lying further to the south (1951-2), and the Wadi En-Nar (Kidron), some seven or eight miles north-east of Bethlehem and west of the Dead Sea (1952). Material recovered from the last two locations is dated about the second century A.D., whereas the Qumran documents probably emerged from the period of the second century B.C. and terminated in the first quarter of the first century A.D.

2. E. Chiera, *They wrote on Clay* (1939), provided a popular account of the excavations at Nuzu. A detailed report was furnished by Chiera in *Joint Expedition with the Iraq Museum at Nuzi* (1927-39), 6 vols., whilst cuneiform texts were also found in R. H. Pfeiffer and E. A. Speiser, *The Annual of the American Schools of Oriental Research* (1935-6), XVI ; *Harvard Semitic Series* (1929), V ; *ibid.* (1932), IX ; *id.* (1942), XII.

3. A. Parrot, *Mari, une ville perdu* (1935), *Syria, Revue d'Art orientale et d'archéologie* (1935), XVI, pp. 1 seq., 117 seq.; *ibid.* (1936), XVII, p. 1 seq.; *id.* (1937), XVIII, pp. 54 seq., 325 seq.; *id.* (1938), XIX, p. 1 seq.; *id.* (1939), XX, p. 1 seq.

4. Howard Carter, *The Tomb of Tut-ankh-Amen* (1923-7), 2 vols.

5. *BDSS*, p. 4.

6. *The Times*, August 9th, 1949. Amongst the numerous publications dealing with the discovery of the scrolls, the following may be noticed here : E. L. Sukenik, *Megilloth Genuzoth* (1948), I, pp. 10 ff., *ibid.* (1950), II, p. 12 seq.; W. F. Albright, *BASOR* (1948), No. 110, p. 2 f.; *ibid.* (1948), No. 111, p. 2 f.; *id.* (1950), No. 118, p. 5 f.; M. Burrows, *JQR* (1949-50), XL, p. 51 seq.; *JBL* (1949), LVIII, p. 195 seq.; W. Baumgartner, *Theologische Rundschau* (1951), N.F.,

XIX, p. 97 seq.; G. R. Driver, *JQR* (1949–50), XL, pp. 127 seq., 359 seq.; R. Gordis, *JNES* (1950), IX, p. 44 seq.; F. F. Bruce, *Journal of the Transactions of the Victoria Institute* (1950), LXXII, p. 131 seq.; P. Kahle, *Die hebräischen Handschriften aus der Höhle* (1951) ; G. R. Driver, *HSDS* (1951) ; A. Michel, *Le Maître de Justice d'après les documents de la Mer Morte, la littérature apocryphe et rabbinique* (1954) ; H. H. Rowley, *The Dead Sea Scrolls and Their Significance* (1955) ; G. Vermès, *Les Manuscrits du Desert de Juda* (1954 ed.) ; J. L. Kelso, *JBL* (1955), LXXIV, p. 141 seq.

7. For earlier Taʿamireh enterprise in cave curios, cf. L–H. Vincent, *RB* (1947), LIV, p. 269.

8. The sheikh to whom the Bedouin had first attempted to sell the scrolls had sent the tribesmen to a Syrian merchant in Bethlehem, one Kalil Eskander. He contacted another Syrian in Jerusalem named George Isaiah, who in turn informed the Metropolitan.

9. *WSDS*, p. 11 f.; *BDSS*, pp. 6 ff. The Metropolitan Samuel's own account of the way in which he acquired the scrolls and sought to determine their nature and content is contained in *BA* (1949), XII, No. 2, p. 26 seq.

10. Wechsler was to become more prominent subsequently when controversy developed about the scrolls.

11. Wechsler first thought that the scrolls were comparatively modern forgeries, but later repudiated this opinion.

12. It will probably appear curious to the reader that Archbishop Samuel had so little awareness of the academic resources around him. Wilson has explained this phenomenon in terms of the lack of communication existing between the various religious denominations of modern Near Eastern Christianity.

13. This man was the one who saw the scrolls at the very beginning, and who had refused to pay the Bedouin £20 for them. Having heard later that the documents were valuable, he purchased the three manuscripts which remained from those offered to the Metropolitan Samuel. Cf. *WSDS*, p. 19.

14. The term *genizah* was used of the store-room of a synagogue in which discarded and dilapidated manuscripts were placed. The veneration and sanctity accorded such synagogue rolls generally precluded disposal by other means. Many scholars have rejected Sukenik's view that the cave had served as a *genizah*, preferring de Vaux's

opinion (*RB* (1949), LVI, p. 236) that the cave was a place of concealment or a secret library. Cf. P. Kahle, *VT* (1951), I, p. 38 seq.

15. *WSDS*, p. 20. For further extracts from his diary, cf. *DSSHU*, p. 17.

16. Sukenik published extracts from the Isaiah manuscript, the War Scroll and the Thanksgiving Hymns in *Megilloth Genuzoth* with the assistance of the Bialik Foundation (Vol. I, 1948 ; Vol. II, 1950). The complete text was edited and published posthumously by the Bialik Foundation and the Hebrew University of Jerusalem under the title *'Oṣar ham-Megilloth hag-Genuzoth she-bidhe ha-Unibhersitah ha-'Ibhrith* in 1954.

17. Its own abbreviated title, *The Rule of War*, is the one by which it is often designated.

18. The Nash Papyrus is a rare Hebrew fragment now in the Library of Cambridge University. Written in an archaic script, it contains the Ten Commandments and the Shema (Deut. 6 : 4 ff.). Professor W. F. Albright took a leading part in establishing a date in the first century B.C. for the fragment, although a few scholars have dated it as late as the second century A.D. Cf. W. F. Albright, *JBL* (1937), LVI, p. 145 seq.; *BASOR* (1949), No. 115, p. 10 seq.; S. A. Cook, *Proceedings of the Society of Biblical Archaeology* (1903), XXV, p. 34 seq.; G. Margoliouth, *Jewish Encyclopedia* (1904), VIII, pp. 304b, 312b.; N. Peters, *Die älteste Abschrift der zehn Gebote, der Papyrus Nash* (1905) ; J. C. Trever, *BASOR* (1949), No. 113, p. 19 ; S. A. Birnbaum, *BASOR* (1949), No. 115, p. 22 ; E. L. Sukenik, *Megilloth Genuzoth* (1948), I, p. 14 ; E. R. Lacheman, *JQR* (1949–50), XL, p. 31.

19. *ADSS*, p. 20 f.; *BDSS*, p. 11 f.

20. Received in Jerusalem on March 15th, 1948.

21. G. E. Wright, *BA* (1948), XI, No. 2, pp. 21 ff. A more extended account of the discovery was published in the next issue, *BA* (1948), XI, No. 3, p. 46 seq.

22. Cf. *BDSS*, p. 14.

23. Cf. M. Burrows, *PEQ* (1950), LXXXII, p. 61 seq.

24. Cf. *BA* (1948), XI, No. 3, p. 50.

25. *DSSMM*, Vol. I, *The Isaiah Manuscript and the Habakkuk Commentary* (1950). Vol. II, Fasc. 2, *Plates and Transcription of the Manual of Discipline* (1951).

26. This so-called " Manual of Discipline " should be more properly styled the *Rule of the Community*.

27. After examining a separate fragment of this tightly-compressed and brittle scroll, Trever concluded that the manuscript was the long-lost apocryphal *Book of Lamech*, but when it was unrolled it proved to be quite different in nature. Cf. J. C. Trever, *BASOR* (1949), No. 115, pp. 8 ff.; *BA* (1956), XIX, No. 1, pp. 22 ff.

28. Cf. G. Lambert, *Revue Générale Belge* (1950), p. 405 seq.

29. *BDSS*, p. 34. The author records (p. 16) that it had been the intention of the American School to visit the site in the Wadi Qumran area during March 1948, but unforeseen circumstances made it impossible for the plan to be carried out.

30. These consisted of bits of newspaper, cigarette stubs and a cigarette roller. The latter bore the name of the owner, and ultimately enabled the authorities to uncover the identity of the marauders. Cf. *ADSS*, p. 26.

31. At first it was thought that all fifty jars had at one time contained scrolls, but this theory was abandoned subsequently.

32. It was probably as a result of these clandestine operations that three fragments of the Book of Daniel were acquired by the Syrian monastery at this time. The scraps of manuscript apparently came from two separate scrolls, and one fragment marked the transition from Hebrew to Aramaic in Dan. 2 : 4.

33. Some scholars have concluded from this evidence that the cave had been entered in the Roman period, and connected the exploit with the tradition preserved by Origen that some Hebrew and Greek manuscripts were found during the reign of Caracalla (A.D. 211–17) in a pottery container not far from Jericho. Cf. P. E. Kahle, *The Cairo Geniza* (1947), p. 161 f.

34. Other fragments from the first Qumran cave which were later acquired by the Palestine Museum included a fragment of the *Rule of the Community*. Cf. R. de Vaux, *RB* (1950), LVII, p. 417 seq.

35. Khirbet Qumran was identified with the location of ancient Gomorrah (F. de Saulcy, *Voyage autour de la Mer morte* (1853), II, pp. 165 ff.), but this was denied by later writers (cf. F. M. Abel, *Une Croisière autour de la Mer morte* (1911), p. 167 f.) ; J. T. Milik (*RB* (1953), LX, p. 538, note 8) held that the area was named after the contemporary designation of the Dead Sea coastal plain, whilst

R. North (*CBQ* (1954), XVI, p. 427) affirmed that the name meant "lunar". The site may be identified tentatively with the "city of Salt" (Joshua 15 : 62).

36. Cf. *BA* (1954), XVII, No. 1, p. 9 f.

37. R. de Vaux, *RB* (1953), LX, p. 245 seq.; cf. F. M. Cross, *BA* (1954), XVII, No. 1, p. 8 seq.

38. *ADSS*, p. 168 f.

39. *ADSS*, p. 170 and pl. 6.

40. One of these documents was published by J. T. Milik, *RB* (1953), LX, p. 276 seq.; cf. J. J. Rabinowitz, *RB* (1954), LXI, p. 191 f.; S. A. Birnbaum, *PEQ* (1954), LXXXVI, p. 23 seq.

41. Cf. G. L. Harding, *PEQ* (1952), LXXXIV, p. 104 seq.; G. L. Harding and W.˙L. Reed, *BA* (1953), XVI, No. 1, p. 25 seq.; R. de Vaux, *RB* (1953), LX, pp. 83 seq., 540 seq.; W. L. Reed, *BASOR* (1954), No. 135, p. 8 seq.

42. Originally the two pieces had been joined together to form one sheet about eight feet in length. Cf. *BA* (1954), XVII, No. 1, p. 7.

43. For a first-hand account of the operation, *vide ADSS*, p. 181 seq.

44. Cf. R. de Vaux, *RB* (1953), LX, p. 85 seq.

45. For a concise account of Nabataean history, cf. J. Starcky, *BA* (1955), XVIII, No. 4, p. 84 seq. The same author has published one of the Nabataean contracts in *RB* (1954), LXI, p. 161 seq. For one of the Aramaic contracts, cf. J. T. Milik, *RB* (1954), LXI, p. 182 seq.

46. *ADSS*, p. 174.

47. McGill University purchased some of the 4Q fragments for $15,000 (cf. R. B. Y. Scott, *BASOR* (1954), No. 135, p. 8), and this example was followed by Manchester University, the Vatican Library, the University of Heidelberg, and other academic institutions. The terms of purchase provided for the fragments to remain at the Palestine Museum until they had been properly identified and published.

48. S. Schechter (ed. and transl.), *Documents of Jewish Sectaries* (1910, 2 vols.). Vol. I, *Fragments of a Zadokite Work*. Cf. *APOT*, Vol. II, p. 785 seq., from which quotations in the present work will be taken. Cf. *etiam* L. Rost, *Die Damaskusschrift neu bearbeitet* (Kleine Texte für Vorlesungen und Uebungen, No. 167), 1933. This Zadokite Fragment is more correctly styled *The Cairo Genizah Document of the*

Damascus Covenanters, and in the present book will be designated CDC (Cairo Damascene Covenanters).

49. July 11th, 1957.

50. The watercourse which lies to the south of this location is the Wadi En-Nar, more familiarly known in antiquity as the brook Kidron. Cf. 2 Sam. 15 : 23 ; 1 Kings 15 : 13 ; Jer. 31 : 40 ; John 18 : 1.

51. This term is employed to describe manuscripts which have been re-used after the original writing has been erased. Frequently the rubbings fail to remove the original script entirely, and in consequence it is often possible to discern what the manuscript contained in the first instance by means of infra-red photography.

52. For a preliminary report, cf. R. de Vaux, *RB* (1953), LX, p. 83 seq.

53. F. de Saulcy, *op. cit.,* II, p. 165 f. Although the modern Bedouin pronunciation of " Qumran " has certain vocal resemblances to " Gomorrah ", there is no etymological connection between them.

54. C. Clermont-Ganneau, *Archaeological Researches in Palestine* (1896), II, p. 14 f. He also repudiated the identification of Khirbet Qumran with Gomorrah.

55. G. Dalman, *PJB* (1914), X, p. 10.; *ibid.* (1920), XVI, p. 40.

56. These latter were replenished during the rainy season.

57. Cf. R. de Vaux, *RB* (1954), LXI, p. 206 seq., for a preliminary account of the investigation.

58. Cf. 2 Chron. 26 : 10.

59. This was the one recorded by Flavius Josephus (*AJ*, XV, 5, 2; cf. *WJ*, I, 19, 3), occurring in the seventh year of Herod the Great (31 B.C.) when he was fighting the Nabataeans near Jericho.

60. *WJ*, IV, 3, 1 f.

61. *ADSS*, p. 89.

62. Cf. 1QS, III : 4 f., 9, V : 13 f. Allegro (*ADSS*, p. 90) questioned the use of the cisterns for baptismal rites. In CDC, XII (*APOT*, II, p. 826), definite regulations were prescribed for ritual purification. Cf. *AJ*, XVIII, 1, 5 ; *WJ*, II, 7, 5.

63. Cf. *RB* (1954), LXI, p. 215 seq.

64. Cf. *RB* (1954), LXI, p. 229.

65. For coins from the first two seasons of work at the site, cf. *RB* (1954), LXI, p. 230 f.

66. Cf. 1QS, VI : 19 f., VII : 25 ; CDC, XVIII in *APOT*, II, p. 832.

67. Clermont-Ganneau, *op. cit.*, II, p. 15 f.

68. Cf. R. de Vaux, *RB* (1953), LX, p. 103. It should be noted that contemporary Jewish graves did not contain funerary offerings.

69. Cf. *VDJD*, p. 17.

70. *WSDS*, p. 120.

71. On arriving in the United States the Metropolitan Samuel assumed the position of Apostolic Delegate to the Syrian Orthodox Congregations in the United States and Canada. At the same time he placed the scrolls in the custody of a Trust, the members of which were Syrians of his own Jacobite Church.

72. June 1st to 3rd, 1954. The advertisement read : " The Four Dead Sea Scrolls. Biblical Manuscripts dating back to at least 200 B.C. are for sale. This would be an ideal gift to an educational or religious institution by an individual or group." Only small sums of money had been realised from exhibiting the manuscripts in various American centres, and the Trust members were anxious to dispose of the scrolls before their value depreciated still further.

73. $150,000 of the total was generously donated by the late Mr. Samuel Gottesman.

74. Y. Yadin, *The Message of the Scrolls* (1957), p. 52.

CHAPTER TWO

1. Cf. *DSSHU*, p. 21.

2. Cf. C. H. Kraeling, *BASOR* (1952), No. 125, p. 6 ; G. R. Driver, *JQR* (1949–50), XL, p. 370 n.

3. Jer. 32 : 14.

4. 1 : 18. *APOT*, II, p. 415. This work was composed in the first century A.D. with the avowed intention of recalling worldly Pharisaism to a fresh observance of the Mosaic Law. The practice of soaking the manuscript in cedar-oil was apparently dictated by a desire to preserve the skin from incidental destruction by insects or rodents. Many of the manuscripts from 4Q had been destroyed by rats and mice because adequate storage precautions had not been taken when the documents were deposited at the site. Why such neglect occurred in some instances is difficult to explain. Cf. *ADSS*, p. 79.

5. Cf. Mrs. G. M. Crowfoot in *PEQ* (1951), LXXXIII, p. 5 seq.; *DJD*, I, Qumran Cave, I, p. 18 seq.; *BDSS*, p. 81. When some of

the Qumran fragments were examined chemically by Dr. H. J. Plenderleith at the British Museum it was discovered that the pitch compound which was thought to have been employed in sealing the earthenware containers originally was in reality nothing more than decayed leather which had become deposited on the jars. Cf. *BA* (1949), XII, No. 3, p. 65.

6. Cf. *DJD*, I, p. 39 f.

7. F. M. Cross, *BA* (1954), XVII, No. 1, p. 15.

8. Cf. *ADSS*, p. 44 seq.

9. " S " is the initial letter of the Hebrew title *Serek ha-yaḥad* (The Order of the Community) as proposed by Sukenik. Burrows had first suggested the title " Manual of Discipline " in 1948. Cf. *BA* (1948), XI, No. 3, p. 57 f.; *BDSS*, p. 24 f.

10. The " p " is an abbreviation of *pesher* or " Commentary ".

11. " H " and " M " represent *Hodayoth* or " Thanksgiving Hymns " and " *Milḥamah* " or " War " respectively. For an earlier system of nomenclature adopted for the scrolls in the possession of the American Schools of Oriental Research, *vide DSSMM*, I, p. xi. What is expected to become the standard nomenclature is found in *DJD*, I, pp. 46 ff.

12. Cf. R. de Vaux, *RB* (1949), LVI, pp. 234 seq., 586 seq.; O. R. Sellers, *BASOR* (1949), No. 114, p. 55 seq.

13. Cf. R. de Vaux, *RB* (1949), LVI, p. 597 seq.; J. T. Milik, *ibid.* (1952), LIX, p. 412 seq.

14. Cf. H. H. Rowley (ed.), *The Old Testament and Modern Study* (1951), p. 24.; S. A. Birnbaum and Y. Yeivin, *BASOR* (1950), No. 118, p. 20 seq.

15. *APOT*, II, p. 6.

16. Cf. C. C. Torrey, *JBL* (1952), LXXI, pp. 39 ff. He points out that translations from Hebrew into Aramaic and *vice versa* were common in the inter-testamental period.

17. The skins had been prepared carefully, and were somewhat of the consistency of parchment, although the present colour of the sheets shows considerable variation. The sheets varied from ten to twenty-five inches in length. Cf. *DSSMM*, I, p. xvii.

18. *DSSMM*, I, p. xiv.

19. *DSSMM*, I, p. xv ; M. Burrows, *BASOR* (1949), No. 113, p. 6 seq.

20. *BDSS*, p. 20.

21. *DSSHU*, fig. 10.

22. Passages of the prophecy extant in 1QISb are : 10 : 17–19 ; 13 : 16–19 ; 16 : 7–11 ; 19 : 20–20 : 1 ; 22 : 24–23 : 4 ; 26 : 1–5 ; 28 : 15–20 ; 29 : 1–8 ; 30 : 10–14 ; 30 : 21–26 ; 35 : 4–5 ; 37 : 8–12 ; 38 : 12–39 : 8 ; 40 : 2–3 ; 41 : 3–23 ; 43 : 1–13 ; 43 : 23–27 ; 44 : 21–45 : 13 ; 46 : 3–47 : 14 ; 48 : 17–49 : 15 ; 50 : 7–51 : 10 52 : 7–54 : 6 ; 55 : 2–57 : 4 ; 57 : 17–59 : 8 ; 59 : 20–61 : 2 ; 62 : 2– 64 : 8 ; 65 : 17–66 : 24.

23. *DSSHU*, figs. 18–21.

24. Cf. W. H. Brownlee, *BASOR* (1948), No. 112, p. 8 seq.

25. DSSMM, I, p. xxi.

26. Many Biblical critics had long maintained that the third chapter of Habakkuk was independent of the first two, and probably a later addition. This need not necessarily imply, however, that it proceeded from a different hand.

27. This monastic community, the Qumran sect, will be discussed more fully in Chapter Five.

28. W. H. Brownlee, *BA* (1951), XIV, No. 3, p. 60 seq., has tabulated some of the interpretative principles recognisable from Rabbinic literature which he also regards as underlying the Commentary.

29. Whilst many scholars translate this phrase literally as the "Teacher of Righteousness", it should actually be rendered the " Right Teacher " or the " Orthodox Teacher ". The present work will employ the designation " Righteous Teacher " in preference to the above. The identity and function of the Teacher will be discussed subsequently.

30. The different views of those who have sought to interpret the events of the Habakkuk Commentary against an historical background are summarised in *VDJD*, pp. 64 ff.

31. *BDSS*, p. 26.

32. I : 1–15.

33. I : 16–II : 18.

34. II : 19–25.

35. II : 25 ; III : 12.

36. III : 13–IV : 26.

37. These rules of discipline dealt with the following topics : social relationships (V : 1–7) ; personal holiness (V : 7–20) ; the procedure

for the examining of postulants (V : 20–4) ; accusations (V : 24–VI : 1) ; communal duties (VI : 1–8) ; the Community Council (VI : 8–13) ; rules concerning initiates and novices (VI : 13–23) ; defections of speech (VI : 23–VII : 5) ; fraudulent behaviour (VIII : 5–8) ; vindictiveness (VII : 8–9) ; indecent talk (VII : 9) ; misbehaviour in public sessions (VII : 9–12) ; indecorous demeanour (VII : 12–15) ; slander (VII : 15–18) ; defection (VII : 18–25) ; appointment of elders (VIII : 1–19) ; demeanour of elders (VIII : 20–IX : 6) ; priestly authority (IX : 7) ; property disposition of elders (IX : 8–11) ; the behaviour of the faithful (IX : 12–16) ; discussion (IX : 16–21) ; loving and hating (IX : 21–6).

38. X–XI.

39. *DSSHU*, p. 37.

40. The fourth sheet was fragmentary, but indicated the existence of three separate columns. Cf. *DSSHU*, fig. 25.

41. *DSSHU*, p. 44.

42. *DSSHU*, p. 37. Certain errors were also corrected by a third hand.

43. *DSSHU*, pl. 39, V : 5 f.

44. *DSSHU*, pl. 39, V : 20 f.

45. *DSSHU*, pl. 38, IV : 8 seq.

46. *GA*, p. 7.

47. Professor Biberkraut had previously opened the first three scrolls acquired by Professor Sukenik.

48. Cf. J. C. Trever, *BASOR* (1948), No. III, p. 6 seq.

49. N. Avigad and Y. Yadin (ed.), *A Genesis Apocryphon* (1956).

50. Cf. J. C. Trever, *BASOR* (1949), No. 115, p. 8 f.

51. Cf. *BDSS*, p. 26.

52. Cf. *APOT*, II, p. 1 seq. Because the extant chapters were concerned with Lamech, Enoch, Noah and Abraham, the scroll was named *A Genesis Apocryphon*.

53. *GA*, p. 8.

54. *GA*, p. 14 f.

55. This narrative is similar to the one concerning Enoch in *APOT*, II, p. 278. A similar fragment in Hebrew was found in 1Q. Cf. *Biblica* (1951), XXXII, p. 393 seq.

56. *GA*, p. 41 f.

57. *GA*, p. 43 f.

58. For a discussion of the identity of these kings, cf. *GA*, p. 34 f.

59. *DSSHU*, p. 35 f. and pls. 16–34.

60. The document may be analysed as follows : Prologue (I : 1–17) ; recruitment (II : 1–9) ; campaigns (II : 9–14) ; trumpet and standard inscriptions (III : 1–IV : 2) ; disposition of infantry and cavalry (IV : 3–VI : 17); age requirements (VII : 1–7) ; battle signals (VII : 8–IX : 15) ; exhortation (X : 1–XII : 18) ; priestly blessing (XIII : 1–XIV : 1) ; victory psalm (XIV : 2–17) ; preparations for battle (XV : 1–XVI : 1) ; instructions for combat (XVI : 2–XVII : 15) ; thanksgiving for victory (XVIII : 1–15). Column XIX is fragmentary.

61. Cf. C. T. Fritsch, *The Qumran Community* (1956), p. 37.

62. Cf. Y. Yadin, *Megillath Milḥamath Bene'Or Bi-Bene Ḥoshekh* (1957 ed.), p. 98 seq.; T. H. Gaster, *The Dead Sea Scriptures in English Translation* (1956), p. 277.

63. G. E. Wright, *BA* (1949), XII, No. 2, p. 33.

64. R. de Vaux reported the preliminary results of decipherment in *RB* (1953), LX, p. 554 f.

65. Cf. *BA* (1956), XIX, No. 4, p. 81 f.

66. These scrolls were discovered on March 20th, 1952. Cf. R. de Vaux, *RB* (1953), LX, p. 84 f.; *ibid.*, p. 540 seq.

67. Cf. K. G. Kuhn, *RB* (1954), LXI, p. 193 seq.

68. Cf. *BA* (1954), XVII, No. 1, p. 6.

69. Cf. *ADSS*, p. 181 seq., for a description of the operation.

70. J. T. Milik, *BA* (1956), XIX, No. 3, p. 62 f.

71. Approximately ten blows of the hammer per letter were required.

72. *BA* (1954), XVII, No. 1, p. 8.

73. A preliminary report on the contents of 4Q appeared in *BA* (1956), XIX, No. 4, p. 83 seq.

74. Cf. *BASOR* (1953), No. 132, p. 15 seq.; *JBL* (1955), LXXIV, p. 147 seq.

75. Cf. *DJD*, I, p. 134.

76. 115a.

77. Probably not much later than A.D. 63.

78. *ADSS*, p. 172.

79. Num. 24 : 17 ff.

80. Literally, " Simon, Son of the Star".

81. That is, "Simon, Son of the Lie".

82. Cf. J. T. Milik, *RB* (1953), LX, p. 276 seq. The Galileans mentioned were probably refugees from the struggle, and may have been Christians, as Milik suggests.

83. Cf. E. Schürer, *Geschichte des jüdischen Volkes im Zeitalter Jesu Christi* (1901–11), 4th ed., I, p. 682, n. 98.

84. The phylactery contained four passages from the Hebrew Torah (Exod. 13 : 1–10, 11–16 ; Deut. 6 : 4–9, 11 : 13–21), which were written in parallel columns on a strip of parchment and placed in a leather container. This was then worn on the left arm or on the forehead in a literal interpretation of Deut. 6 : 6–8. From the remains of the Qumran phylacteries it is apparent that they included the Decalogue as well as the above passages. This type of phylactery was already obsolescent in the time of Christ. Cf. *RB* (1953), LX, p. 268 f.

85. *RB* (1953), LX, p. 18 seq.

86. *Dialogue with Trypho, a Jew*, LXXI.

87. Cf. *ADSS*, pp. 177 ff.

88. An interim list of such fragments is contained in *VDJD*, p. 25 seq.

CHAPTER THREE

1. For a brief account of this process, *vide ADSS*, pp. 50 ff.

2. F. Kenyon, *Our Bible and the Ancient Manuscripts* (1939 ed.), p. 48. Before he died (August 23rd, 1952) he recognised the genuine nature and pre-Masoretic date of the Qumran scrolls.

3. A number of works which are alleged to be literary forgeries from this period have been examined by J. Carter and G. Pollard in *An Enquiry Into the Nature of Certain Nineteenth Century Pamphlets* (1934), p. 8 seq. In the middle of the nineteenth century a certain Constantine Simonides endeavoured to pass off several faked fragments of early New Testament writings as genuine but without success, and was exposed by Tischendorf.

4. Cf. G. Lambert, *NRTh* (1949), p. 286. A more recent New Testament literary fraud which was mercifully short in duration and localised in area was reported to the present writer under the title of the *Partridge Manuscript*. The Piltdown fiasco is an example of the

way in which hoaxes have been perpetrated successfully in the scientific field. Cf. J. S. Weiner, *The Piltdown Forgery* (1955).

5. Amongst those adopting this view were B. Reicke, *Studia Theologica* (1949), II, fasc. I, p. 45 seq. (subsequently abandoned in *Handskrifterna Från Qumran* (1952) ; G. Lambert, *NRTh* (1952), LXXIV, p. 259 seq.; H. H. Rowley, *ZFDSS*, p. 62 seq.; A. Michel, *Le Maître de Justice d'après les documents de la Mer Morte* (1954), p. 232 seq.

6. Cf. R. de Vaux, *RB* (1950), LVII, p. 428 f.; *ibid.* (1951), LVIII, p. 442 f.; M. Delcor, *Les Manuscrits de la Mer Morte : Essai sur le Midrash d'Habacuc* (1951), p. 56 seq.; Delcor, *RB* (1951), LVIII, p. 521 seq.; *ibid.*, *Revue de l'Histoire des Religions* (1952), CXLII, p. 129 seq.

7. Cf. J. van der Ploeg, *BO* (1951), VIII, p. 9 f.; M. H. Segal, *JBL* (1951), LXX, p. 131 seq.; W. H. Brownlee, *BA* (1951), XIV, No. 3, p. 63.; D. Barthélemy, *RB* (1952), LIX, p. 207 seq.

8. Cf. A. Dupont-Sommer, *Revue de l'Histoire des Religions* (1950), CXXXVII, p. 129 seq.; *ibid.*, *Observations sur le Commentaire d'Habacuc découvert près de la Mer Morte* (1950) ; *APMMM*, p. 40.; R. Goosens, *La Nouvelle Clio* (1949–50), I–II, pp. 336 seq., 634 seq.; *ibid.* (1951–2), III–IV, p. 137 seq.; K. Elliger, *Studien zum Habakuk-Kommentar vom Toten Meer* (1953), p. 226 seq.; F. F. Bruce, *Second Thoughts on the Dead Sea Scrolls* (1956), pp. 72 ff., 138. Dupont-Sommer at first identified the Kittim of 1QM with the Seleucids and the Kittim of 1QpHab with the Romans (cf. *APMMM*, p. 98), but now thinks that the Kittim of 1QM are Roman forces also. Cf. *Revue de l'Histoire des Religions* (1955), CXLVIII, p. 42 f.

9. Cf. J. L. Teicher, *JJS* (1951), II, p. 67 seq.; *ibid.* (1952), III, p. 53 seq.; R. Tournay, *RB* (1949), LVI, p. 204 seq.; G. Vermès, *Ephemerides Theologicae Lovanienses* (1951), XXVII, p. 70 seq. (cf. *Cahiers Sioniens* (1953), p. 3 seq.).

10. Cf. P. R. Weis, *JQR* (1950–1), XLI, p. 125 seq.; S. Zeitlin, *ibid.* (1950–1), XLI, p. 251 seq.

11. H. L. Ginsberg, *BASOR* (1948), No. 112, p. 20.

12. R. de Vaux, *RB* (1950), LVII, p. 428 f., *et al.*

13. Cf. *APMMM*, p. 38 seq.; R. Tournay, *RB* (1949), LVI, p. 232 ; P. Kahle, *VT* (1951), I, p. 43 f.; R. Marcus, *JNES* (1951), X, p. 281 seq.

14. Cf. S. Zeitlin, *JQR* (1950–1), XLI, p. 32 seq.; P. R. Weis, *ibid.* (1950–1), XLI, p. 125 seq.

15. Cf. G. Vermès, *Cahiers Sioniens* (1950), p. 198, where the period of composition was assigned to A.D. 70–90 ; A. Dupont-Sommer, *Semitica* (1957), VII, p. 10.

16. Cf. *ZFDSS*, p. 83.

17. For a date between 65 and 63 B.C., cf. *VDJD*, p. 84.

18. *BDSS*, p. 118 f.; Y. Yadin, *Megillath Milḥamath Bene 'Or Bi-Bene Ḥoshekh*, pp. 222 ff.

19. *BASOR* (1950), No. 118, p. 6.

20. *BASOR* (1949), No. 113, p. 23.

21. *BASOR* (1949), No. 115, p. 22.

22. *Megilloth Genuzoth*, I, p. 14 f.

23. Cf. R. de Vaux, *RB* (1949), LVI, pp. 234, 586 seq.; G. L. Harding, *PEQ* (1949), LXXXI, p. 113. Dupont-Sommer questioned such a precise dating as this in *APMMM*, pp. 21, 43, and in *Revue de Paris*, July 1949, p. 87. Cf. W. F. Albright, *BASOR* (1949), No. 115, p. 13n., and *The Old Testament and Modern Study* (1951), p. 23.

24. R. de Vaux, *RB* (1949), LVI, p. 586 seq.; cf. *ADSS*, p. 77 f.

25. *ADSS*, p. 79.

26. For a comprehensive study of this area of scientific discovery, cf. W. F. Libby, *Radiocarbon Dating* (1954). Carbon-14 function is also discussed in K. Rankana, *Isotope Geology* (1954), p. 181 seq.

27. Cf. A. Bauchau, *NRTh* (1950), LXXII, pp. 515 ff.; D. Collier, *BA* (1951), XIV, No. 1, p. 25 seq.; G. E. Wright, *ibid.* (1951), XIV, No. 1, pp. 31 ff.; W. G. Guindon, *CBQ* (1951), XIII, p. 265 seq.; E. S. Deevy, *The Scientific American*, February 1952, p. 24 seq.; *ADSS*, pp. 80 ff.; M. Wheeler, *Archaeology from the Earth* (1956), pp. 50 ff.

28. Cf. O. R. Sellers, *BASOR* (1951), No. 123, pp. 24 ff.; *BA* (1951), XIV, No. 1, p. 29.

29. Cf. R. de Vaux, *RB* (1954), LXI, p. 206 seq.

30. February 15th to April 15th, 1954.

31. *ADSS*, p. 89 and pls. 36, 37.

32. Some of these coins have been tabulated in *VDJD*, p. 16.

33. *RB* (1949), LVI, p. 236.

34. *HSDS*, p. 50.

35. Cf. R. de Vaux, *RB* (1956), LXIII, p. 567.

CHAPTER FOUR

1. For a discussion of its canonicity, cf. L. B. Paton, The Book of Esther in I.C.C. (1908), pp. 94 ff.

2. *BDSS*, p. 106 ; *BASOR* (1948), No. 111, pp. 20, 22 ; *ibid.* (1949), No. 113, p. 25.

3. In 1QISa, 16 : 8, twenty words were omitted after " wine of Sibmah ", the text being resumed after the same phrase in 16 : 9. Cf. *DSSMM*, I, pl. XIII, line 26.

4. E.g. W. Robertson Smith, *The Prophets of Israel* (1895), p. 355.

5. Cf. G. B. Gray, Isaiah I in I.C.C. (1912), pp. lvi, 332 seq., 397 seq.; C. F. Kent, *The Sermons, Epistles and Apocalypses of Israel's Prophets* (1910), p. 497 f.

6. On this basis the suggestion made by Dupont-Sommer which related the experience of the Suffering Servant to that of the Righteous Teacher is obviously fanciful. Cf. *D-SDSS*, p. 96.

7. Cf. R. H. Pfeiffer, *Introduction to the Old Testament* (1941), p. 598 ; W. H. Ward, Habakkuk in I.C.C. (1911), p. 6 ; S. R. Driver, *Introduction to the Literature of the Old Testament* (1898), p. 339.

8. *BA* (1949), XII, No. 2, p. 33.

9. Cf. Pfeiffer, *op. cit., supra.*, 765 f.; Driver, *op. cit., supra.*, p. 497 seq.; J. A. Montgomery, Daniel in I.C.C. (1927), pp. 96 ff.

10. 1QS, I : 1 seq.

11. Cf. 1QS, V : 3 f.

12. Cf. 1QS, VI : 6 ff., IX : 13 f., X : 1 ff., 10.

13. W. H. Brownlee, *BA* (1951), XIV, No. 3, p. 54.

14. 1QpHab, VII : 3 ff.

15. 1QS, V : 1 ff.

16. Cf. Mark 7 : 9 seq.

17. 1QS, V : 13 f.

18. Cf. 1QS, VIII : 15.

19. 1QS, III : 1 seq.

20. 1QS, V : 7 seq.; cf. 1QS, II : 17.

21. 1QS, IX : 9 f.

22. 1QS, VIII : 21 seq.

23. W. H. Brownlee, *BA* (1951), XIV, No. 3, p. 60. Cf. 1QS, VIII : 11 f.

24. Cf. M. Delcor, *RB* (1951), LVIII, p. 521 seq.

25. 1QpHab, VIII : 1 ff.

26. 1QpHab, XI : 4 f.; cf. CDC, IX : 29 B.

27. 1QpHab, VIII : 8 seq., 16 seq.; IX : 8 seq.

28. For a discussion of the identity of this group, *vide VDJD*, pp. 78 seq., 89 seq.

29. Cf. Isa. 23 : 1, 12 ; Jer. 2 : 10 ; Ezek. 27 : 6. The "ships of Kittim " alluded to in Num. 24 : 25 and Dan. 11 : 30 may have indicated a mercantile or naval group in the Mediterranean.

30. Cf. *Megilloth Genuzoth*, I, p. 18.

31. E.g. R. de Vaux. *RB* (1951), LVIII, p. 442.; M. Delcor, *ibid.*, p. 525 f.; Delcor, *Essai sur le Midrash d'Habacuc* (1951), p. 40 f.

32. Cf. 1 Macc. 1 : 1, 8 : 5 ; Jub. 24 : 28 f., 37 : 10.

33. 1QpHab, III : 10 f.

34. J. van der Ploeg, *BO* (1951), VIII, p. 10, and M. H. Segal, *JBL* (1951), LXX, p. 134, proposed the identification of the "guilty house" with the Roman proconsuls and the Senate.

35. 1QpHab, VI : 4 f. Cf. A. A. Dupont-Sommer, *Revue de l'Histoire des Religions* (1950), CXXXVII, p. 159.

36. For the suggestion that this was practised by the Greeks and other peoples in the east, cf. *ZFDSS*, p. 73 f.; *PEQ* (1956), LXXXVIII, pp. 102 ff.

37. R. Goosens, *La Nouvelle Clio* (1951–2), III–IV, p. 137 seq.

38. *WJ*, VI, 6, 1.

39. *Vide BDSS*, p. 172 seq., for a survey of the problems connected with the identification of the Wicked Priest. For various theories regarding the historical background of 1QpHab, cf. W. H. Brownlee, *BASOR* (1952), No. 126, p. 10 seq.

40. 1QS, IX : 11.

41. CDC, XII : 23 seq., XIV : 19, XIX : 10 f., XX : 1. The singular form of the title may be due to scribal emendation. Cf. J. T. Milik, *RB* (1953), LX, p. 291.

42. *APOT*, II, p. 294.

43. Cf. K. G. Kuhn, *New Testament Studies* (1955), I, p. 168 seq.

44. Cf. *ADSS*, pp. 138 ff.

45. Deut. 18 : 18 f. This passage was followed in the Qumran *florilegium* by Deut. 5 : 28 f.

46. Num. 24 : 15 ff.

47. Deut. 33 : 8 seq. A quotation from an hitherto unknown pseudepigraphal work concluded the document.

48. For a free translation, *vide* T. H. Gaster, *op. cit.*, p. 307 seq. Cf. D. Barthélemy, *RB* (1952), LIX, pp. 203 ff.; *ADSS*. p. 115.

49. *RB* (1953), LX, p. 291.

50. Ezek. 45–6.

51. Cf. J. van der Ploeg, *BO* (1951), VIII, p. 13.

52. Cf. W. H. Brownlee, *United Presbyterian* (1953), November 30, December 7, 14, 21, 28.

CHAPTER FIVE

1. The origin of the term is obscure. For an etymological discussion, *vide* K. Cook, *The Fathers of Jesus* (1886), II, p. 48 f.

2. *Hist. Nat.*, V, 15 (Loeb Class. Lib. Trans., II, p. 277).

3. *D-SDSS*, p. 86n.

4. *Every Good Man is Free*. This was probably written in the first decade of the first century A.D.

5. Philo, *op. cit.*, XII (Loeb Class. Lib. Trans., IX, p. 53 seq.).

6. Cf. Eusebius, *Praeparatio Evangelica*, VIII : 5, 11.

7. Not all Essene groups shared this view, however, as will appear subsequently.

8. *Hypothetica*, XI (Loeb Class. Lib. Trans., IX, p. 437 seq.).

9. For the esteem in which Herod the Great held the Essenes, cf. *AJ*, XV : 10, 4.

10. "When I was about sixteen years old I had a mind to make trial of the several sects that were among us . . . for I thought that by this means I might choose the best, if I were once acquainted with them all ; so I contented myself with hard fare, and underwent great difficulties, and went through them all." *The Life of Flavius Josephus*, Sect. 1.

11. *WJ*, II, 8, 2 seq.

12. *AJ*, XVIII, 1, 5.

13. Hippolytus, *The Refutation of All Heresies*, IX, 13 seq. (Trans. in *The Ante-Nicene Fathers* (1886), V, p. 134 f.).

14. Probably Josephus had in mind the saying of morning prayers at sunrise rather than actual sun-worship.

15. *De Vita Contemplativa* (Loeb. Class. Lib. Trans., IX, p. 113 seq.).

16. Eusebius (*Hist. Eccles.*, II, 17) held that this community con-

stituted the first generation of converts to Christianity resulting from the evangelistic work of St. Mark in Alexandria.

17. *De Vita Contemplativa*, XXV seq. (Loeb. Class. Lib. Trans., IX, p. 127 seq.).

18. Two recent English editions of the text, with translation and notes are, S. Zeitlin, *The Zadokite Fragments* (*Jewish Quarterly Review*, Monograph Series, No. 1, 1952), and C. Rabin, *The Zadokite Documents*, 1954.

19. In fulfilment of Num. 24 : 17.

20. *DSSET*, pp. 4, 101 n. 23.

21. *PEQ* (1955), LXXXVII, p. 34.

22. E.g. D. Howlett, *The Essenes and Christianity* (1957), p. 116.

23. Cf. W. H. Brownlee, *BA* (1950), XIII, No. 3, p. 51.

24. This rendering follows the confession employed on the Day of Atonement. Cf. Ps. 106 : 6.

25. The confession in Dan. 10 appears to preserve a genuine Exilic tradition, and is probably roughly contemporary.

26. *BA* (1950), XIII, No. 3, p. 53.

27. By employing the ancient *Atbash* cipher, H. J. Schonfield (*Secrets of the Dead Sea Scrolls*, 1956, p. 3) converted the word *Hagu* into Tsaraph, or " The Refiner ". This he regarded as an alternative designation of the Righteous Teacher, who would thus appear as the Refiner of Malachi 3 : 2 f. This contention may be supported further by the presence of Metsareph in 1QS, VIII : 4.

28. Cf. 1QS, VI : 3 and CDC, XVII : 5.

29. Cf. R. de Vaux, *RB* (1950), LVII, p. 417 seq. ; D. Barthélemy, *ibid.* (1952), LIX, p. 187 seq.

30. The fragments also mentioned the position of women in the community.

31. S. Schechter, *op. cit.*, I, p. xvi.

32. Cf. CDC, VI : 1, VIII : 6, 15, IX : 5, 8, 28, 37.

33. M. Burrows, *OS* (1950), VIII, p. 184. Cf. *DSSMM*, I, p. x.

34. Cf. *ZFDSS*, p. 76.

35. *APOT*, II, p. 790.

36. These two Teachers were differentiated by L. Rost, *Theologische Literaturzeitung* (1953), LXXVIII, cols. 143 ff., but were identified by R. H. Charles, *APOT*, II, p. 800 f., and Dupont-Sommer, *APMMM*, p. 78.

37. Dupont-Sommer (*JSQE*, p. 55) regarded the titles "Righteous Teacher" and "Messiah" as the incarnate and divine aspects of one individual. Attempts to interpret the CDC references in the light of corresponding sections of 1QpHab generally prove inconclusive. Cf. W. H. Brownlee, *BASOR* (1952), No. 126, p. 10 seq. Perhaps the period just prior to the capture of Jerusalem by Roman forces in 63 B.C. is the one which the writer of 1QpHab described. Cf. F. F. Bruce, *op. cit.*, p. 91 seq.

38. The Rabbinic lunar calendar comprised thirteen months of twenty-eight days each.

39. *APOT*, II, p. 22.

40. *APOT*, II, p. 237 seq. For a discussion of calendaric elements in the Qumran scrolls, cf. J. Obermann, *JBL* (1956), LXXV, p. 285 seq.

41. This dualism has much in common with that found in such books as *Enoch, Jubilees*, the *Testament of the Twelve Patriarchs*, issuing from the intertestamental period, and the *Two Ways* from the early Christian era.

42. Cf. J. B. Noss, *Man's Religions* (1949), p. 450 seq.; K. G. Kuhn, *Zeitschrift für Theologie und Kirche* (1952), XLIX, p. 245 seq.; *JSQE*, p. 118 seq.

43. *WJ*, II, 18, 8.

44. *WJ*, II, 8, 5.

45. Cf. C. Rabin, *Qumran Studies*, Scripta Judaica II (1957), p. 8 seq.

46. Cf. 1QS, VII : 2, 16 f., 24 f.

47. 1QS, VII : 9 f. prescribed a fine for violation of this regulation.

48. *WJ*, II, 7, 9.

49. Cf. *WJ*, II, 8, 2.

50. *WJ*, II, 8, 13. Cf. 1QS, IV : 7 and CDC, IX : 1. The remains of female skeletons from the Qumran cemetery would seem to indicate that women were numbered amongst the sectaries, and is in accord with the provisions in CDC, VII : 1 seq. G. Graystone, *The Dead Sea Scrolls and the Originality of Christ* (1956), p. 103, has suggested that such burials either indicated an earlier stage in the history of the Qumran sect, or that the burial of devout women at the site was sanctioned by the community. In view of the absence of regulations in 1QS regarding celibacy it is doubtful if the sect actually passed

through the kind of evolutionary phase which resulted in women being excluded. If the community was celibate by nature, it is difficult to see why the custom of burying pious women within its sacred precincts should have arisen in the first place.

51. Josephus is not clear about this matter. Cf. *AJ*, XVIII, 1, 5.

52. Those adopting this view include J. Trinquet, *VT* (1951), I, pp. 287 ff. ; G. Lambert, *NRTh* (1952), LXXIV, p. 271 seq. ; H. H. Rowley, *ZFDSS*, p. 62 seq. ; H. Bardtke, *Die Handschriftenfunde am Toten Meer* (1952), p. 143 seq. ; H. H. Rowley, *Bulletin of the John Rylands Library* (1957), XL, p. 137 seq.

53. Cf. Burrows, *OS* (1950), VIII, p. 189.

54. For some who have adopted this view, *vide* R. de Vaux, *RB* (1950), LVII, p. 428 f. ; M. H. Segal, *JBL* (1951), LXX, p. 131 seq. ; D. Barthélemy, *RB* (1952), LIX, p. 207 seq. ; W. H. Brownlee, *BA* (1951), XIV, No. 3, p. 63.

55. Cf. A. Dupont-Sommer, *APMMM*, p. 49 seq. ; R. Goosens, *La Nouvelle Clio* (1949–50), I–II, pp. 336 ff, proposed the identification of Onias with the Righteous Teacher. Cf. R. Goosens, *Bulletin de l'Académie Royale de Belgique* (Classe de Lettres), Fifth Ser. (1950), XXXVI, pp. 440 ff.

56. In *Revue Archéologique*, Sixth Ser. (1949), XXXIV, p. 80, Dupont-Sommer had maintained that the Kittim of the Habakkuk Commentary, which he at that time dated from the period of the Maccabees, were Greek forces.

57. *BASOR* (1952), No. 126, p. 10 seq. Cf. M. H. Segal, *JBL* (1951), LXX, p. 134 f.

58. Cf. *APMMM*, pp. 112 ff.

59. *ZFDSS*, p. 82 ; cf. G. Molin, *Judaica* (1951), VII, p. 193 ; W. Baumgartner, *Theologische Rundschau* (1951), XIX, p. 140 f.

60. *AJ*, XIII, 5, 9.

61. Cf. F. F. Bruce, *op. cit.*, p. 121.

62. Cf. C. T. Fritsch, *op. cit.*, p. 110.

63. W. H. Brownlee, *The Dead Sea Manual of Discipline* (*BASOR* Suppl. Stud. X–XII (1951), p. 4), supports this hypothesis.

64. *AJ*, XV, 10, 4.

65. *APMMM*, pp. 111 ff. ; *NASMMM*, p. 153 seq.

66. *VDJD*, p. 61.

67. C. Rabin, *Qumran Studies*, pp. 59 f., 69 f.
68. According to R. Marcus, *JBL* (1954), LXXIII, p. 161, the Qumran sectaries were gnosticising Pharisees, but less heretical than the Minim who were condemned by the Tannaite authorities.
69. Cf. Schechter, *op. cit.*, I, xviii seq.
70. Cf. L. Nemoy, *Hebrew Union College Annual* (1930), VII, p. 326 seq.
71. Cf. Nemoy, *op. cit., supra.*, p. 363 f.
72. Cf. R. de Vaux, *RB* (1950), LVII, p. 417 seq.
73. Cf *HSDS*, p. 25 f.
74. Cf. *ZFDSS*, p. 24.
75. *ZFDSS*, p. 26.
76. O. Cullmann in *Neutestamentliche Studien presented to R. Bultmann* (1954), p. 35 seq.
77. *JJS* (1951), II, pp. 67 seq., 115 seq.

CHAPTER SIX

1. Cf. *APMMM*, p. 121.
2. *WSDS*, p. 114.
3. IX : 11. Cf. CDC, IX : 10B, XV : 4.
4. Acts 3 : 22, 7 : 37.
5. John 1 : 21.
6. Matt. 17 : 10 ; Mark 9 : 11.
7. John 6 : 14.
8. These are generally held to be : 42 : 1–4 or perhaps 1–9 ; 49 : 1–6 or possibly 1–13 ; 50 : 4–9 or perhaps 4–11 ; 52 : 13–53 : 12.
9. 1QS, VIII : 1.
10. 1QS, VIII : 4 seq.
11. IV : 22.
12. Cf. Is. 42 : 6 ; 49 : 8.
13. IV : 20 ff.
14. Cf. W. H. Brownlee, *BASOR* (1953), No. 132, pp. 10 ff.
15. Cf. R. Eisler, *Modern Churchman* (1949), XXXIX, p. 284 seq.
16. *APMMM*, p. 121 ; *D-SDSS*, p. 99.
17. Cf. *JSQE*, p. 160 seq.
18. *VT* (1951), I, p. 200 seq. ; *D-SDSS*, p. 34.
19. Published by Allegro in *JBL* (1956), LXXV, p. 89 seq.

20. C. Rabin, *JJS* (1956), VII, p. 11 seq., followed Allegro in this identification.

21. Cf. *AJ*, XIII, 14, 1 f. ; *WJ*, I, 4, 6.

22. *ADSS*, p. 95 seq. ; *JBL* (1956), LXXV, p. 89 seq.

23. Cf. T. H. Gaster, *DSSET*, p. 26.

24. Cf. W. H. Brownlee, *BA* (1950), XIII, No. 3, p. 69 seq. ; *ibid.*, *Interpretation* (1955), IX, p. 71 seq. ; B. Reike, *Religion och Bibel* (1952), XI, p. 5 seq. ; A. S. Geyser, *NT* (1956), p. 70 seq. ; E. Stauffer, *Theologische Literaturzeitung* (1956), LXXXI, col. 143 f. ; *ADSS*, p. 163 seq.

25. 1QS, X : 20, 1 ; CDC, II : 3, IX : 41.

26. CDC, IX : 15.

27. 1QS, III : 6 seq., V : 13 f.

28. Cf. 1QS, VIII : 12 ff.

29. Cf. 1QS, IV : 21 ; CDC, II : 10.

30. Cf. 1QH, III : 25 seq.

31. CDC, IX : 10, 29 ; XV : 4 ; XVIII : 8.

32. Cf. 1QS, VIII : 13 f.

33. *DJD*, I, p. 108 seq.

34. Cf. *WJ*, II, 8, 2.

35. Cf. 1QS, VI : 3 ; CDC, XV : 5.

36. Cf. J. A. T. Robinson, *Harvard Theological Review* (1957), I, No. 3, p. 177 ; *ADSS*, p. 164.

37. Cf. John 1 : 35 ; W. H. Brownlee, *BA* (1950), XIII, No. 3, p. 72 ; J. A. T. Robinson, *op. cit.*, *supra*, p. 190.

38. Cf. W. H. Brownlee, *Interpretation* (1955), IX, p. 89, and the revised form of the article in K. Stendahl (Ed.), *The Scrolls and the New Testament* (1957), p. 33 seq. Cf. *BDSS*, p. 340 f.

39. Cf. K. G. Kuhn, *Zeitschrift für Theologie und Kirche* (1950), XLVII, p. 209 f. ; W. Grossouw, *Studia Catholica* (1951), XXVI, p. 295 seq. ; L. Mowry, *BA* (1954), XVII, No. 4, p. 78 seq. ; F. M. Braun, *RB* (1955), LXII, p. 5 seq. ; O. Cullmann, *JBL* (1955), LXXIV, p. 213 seq. ; W. F. Albright in *The Background of the New Testament and its Eschatology* (1956), p. 163 seq.

40. Cf. 1QS, I : 9 f.

41. John 14 : 17, 15 : 26, 16 : 13 ; 1 John 4 : 6. Cf. 1QS, III : 13– IV : 26.

42. John 8 : 12, 11 : 10, 12 : 35 ; 1 John 1 : 6 f., 2 : 11. Cf. 1QS, III : 20 f.

43. John 8 : 12. Cf. 1QS, III : 15.
44. John 6 : 28, 9 : 3. Cf. 1QS, IV : 4.
45. Cf. K. G. Kuhn, *Zeitschrift für Theologie und Kirche* (1950), XLVII, p. 192 seq. ; *ibid.* (1952), XLIX, p. 245 seq.
46. For four principal ways in which Johannine teaching differed from Essenism, cf. W. F. Albright in *The Background of the New Testament and its Eschatology*, p. 170.
47. Kirsopp Lake, *An Introduction to the New Testament* (1937), p. 53.
48. For an examination of the relationship between the Qumran texts and Matt. 5–7, *vide* K. Schubert, *Theologische Quartalschrift* (1955), CXXXV, p. 320 seq.
49. Cf. H. Strack and P. Billerbeck, *Kommentar zum Neuen Testament aus Talmud und Midrasch* (1922–8), 4 vols. ; C. G. Montefiore, *Commentary on the Synoptic Gospels* (1927) ; *ibid.*, *Rabbinic Literature and Gospel Teachings* (1930) ; D. Daube, *The New Testament and Rabbinic Judaism* (1956), p. 55 seq.
50. 1QS, V : 25 seq.
51. 1QS, III : 6 f.
52. Cf. 1QS, II : 8, IV : 2 seq. ; 1QpHab, V : 4.
53. 1QS, VIII : 4 seq.
54. 1QS, IV : 22.
55. Cf. H. L. Ginsberg, *VT* (1953), III, p. 400 seq. ; M. Delcor, *Recherches de Science Religieuse* (1952), XCIV, p. 363 seq.
56. 1QS, VIII : 1. Cf. 1QS, VI : 19.
57. The three priests may be reminiscent of the three " pillars " of the Church in Gal. 2 : 9.
58. The equivalent of *paqidh* in 1QS, VI : 14.
59. The relegation of the Pastoral Epistles to the second quarter of the second century A.D. on the ground that the ecclesiastical organisation which they depict is too advanced for the Apostolic Age is now shown by the scrolls to be totally unwarranted.
60. Cf. CDC, XIII : 7 seq.
61. Cf. Isa. 58 : 6, 61 : 1 ; Ezek. 34 : 12. In Isa. 40 : 11 God is spoken of as feeding His flock like a shepherd.
62. 1 Cor. 4 : 1.
63. Acts 2 : 42 ; 2 Cor. 6 : 14 ; Phil. 1 : 5.
64. 1QS, II : 24 f.

65. 1QS, VI : 2 f.
66. 1QS, I : 11 f. Cf. 1QS, V : 2.
67. *WJ*, II, 8, 3.
68. 1QS, VI : 19 f.
69. 1QS, VI : 21 f.
70. Acts 4 : 32.
71. Acts 2 : 44 f., 4 : 32 seq.
72. Acts 4 : 34, 37, 5 : 1.
73. Acts 5 : 4.
74. Cf. CDC, XIV : 12 ff.
75. 1QS, III : 4 seq.
76. 1QS, V : 13 f.
77. Cf. 1QS, III : 6 seq., IV : 20 ff.
78. 1QS, IV : 21 f.
79. Cf. 1QS, IX : 11 ; CDC, II : 9.
80. Isa. 52 : 15. Cf. John 1 : 33.
81. 1QS, VI : 2 seq.
82. *WJ*, II, 8, 5.
83. Acts 2 : 42, 20 : 7.
84. 1 Cor. 11 : 20 seq.
85. Luke 22 : 18, 29 f. For parallels to the Messianic repast in Rabbinic literature, *vide* J. Bloch, *On the Apocalypse in Judaism* (*JQR*, Monograph Series, No. 2), 1952, p. 96 seq.
86. John 13 : 21 seq.
87. 1QS, VI : 10.
88. Luke 22 : 24.
89. Cf. K. G. Kuhn, *Evangelische Theologie* (1950), X, p. 508 seq. Kuhn rightly differentiates between the earliest forms of the Lord's Supper and the later Eucharistic developments.
90. Matt. 26 : 17 f. ; Mark 14 : 12 ; Luke 22 : 8.
91. Cf. Heb. 10 : 1 seq.
92. Aboth, V : 10.
93. *WJ*, VI, 9, 3.
94. Cf. *VDJD*, p. 48 seq. ; S. Lieberman, *JBL* (1952), LXXI, p. 199 seq.
95. This can be paralleled from Rabbinic literature and the writings of the Early Fathers.
96. Matt. 2 : 6.

97. Cf. *ADSS*, p. 137.

98. Cf. Eusebius, *Hist. Eccles.*, III, 39.

99. J. Rendel Harris in his *Testimonies*, 2 vols. (1916–20).

100. E.g. Rom. 6 : 19, 7 : 5, 18, 25, 8 : 3 seq. ; 2 Cor. 1 : 17, 5 : 16, 10 : 2 f. ; Gal. 5 : 13, 16 seq., 6 : 8 ; Eph 2 : 3 ; Col. 2 : 11, 13, 18.

101. E.g. 1QpHab, IX : 3 ; 1QS, III : 6 ff., XI : 9 ; 1QM, IV : 3.

102. Cf. 1QS, III : 13–IV : 26.

103. 1QS, II : 2.

104. 1QS, IV : 1 seq.

105. Cf. Rom. 1 : 29 ff., 13 : 13 ; Gal. 5 : 19 f. ; Col. 3 : 5, 8.

106. As in Rom. 3–5 ; Gal. 2 : 16–3 : 29 ; Eph. 2 : 8 *et al.*

107. 1QH, I : 26 f., IV : 30 f., 40 *et al.*

108. 1QS, XI : 2 f., 13 ff.

109. 1QpHab, VIII : 1 seq.

110. Cf. 1QS, VIII : 4 ; 1QH, II : 35, VIII : 26 seq., IX : 6 seq., XI : 19 seq.

111. 1QS, IV : 7 f. The concept of a " crown of glory " was also prominent in Mandaean liturgical compositions.

112. Cf. 1QH, III : 23 seq., V : 8.

113. 1QS, IV : 9 seq.

114. Cf. *DSSET*, p. 16 f.

115. Presumably the *Assumption of Moses* and the *Book of Enoch*. For parallels between these works and certain New Testament compositions, cf. *APOT*, II, p. 412 f., 428.

116. As preserved by Eusebius, *Hist. Eccles.*, IV, 22. " The following were those that were opposed to the tribe of Judah and the Christ : Essenes, Galileans, Hemerobaptists, Masbothaeans, Samaritans, Sadducees, Pharisees." (Quoted from *The Nicene and Post-Nicene Fathers* (1890), I, p. 199 f.) Justin (*Dialog.*, LXXX) mentioned seven Jewish sects in this connection, but did not include the Essenes.

117. *The New Republic*, April 9th, 1956, p. 19.

SHORT BIBLIOGRAPHY

Albright, W. F., " On the Date of the Scrolls from ʿAin Feshkha and the Nash Papyrus ", *BASOR* (1949), No. 115, p. 10 seq.

The Archaeology of Palestine, 1949.

" Are the ʿAin Feshkha Scrolls a Hoax ? ", *JQR* (1949–50), XL, p. 41 seq.

" The Chronology of the Dead Sea Scrolls " in W. H. Brownlee, *The Dead Sea Manual of Discipline* (1951), p. 57 seq.

" New Light on Early Recensions of the Hebrew Bible ", *BASOR* (1955), No. 140, p. 27 seq.

Allegro, J. M., " A newly Discovered Fragment of a Commentary on Psalm 37 from Qumrân ", *PEQ* (1954), LXXXVI, p. 69 seq.

" Some Archaeological Sites and the Old Testament : Qumrân ", *The Expository Times* (1955), LXVII, p. 259 seq.

The Dead Sea Scrolls, 1956.

Avigad, N., and Yadin, Y., *A Genesis Apocryphon*, 1956.

Bardtke, H., *Die Handschriftenfunde am Toten Meer*, 1952.

Barthélemy, D., " Le Grand Rouleau d'Isaie trouvé près de la Mer Morte ", *RB* (1950), LVII, p. 530 seq.

" Notes en marge de publications récentes sur les manuscrits de Qumran ", *RB* (1952), LIX, p. 187 seq.

" Redécouverte d'un chaînon manquant de l'histoire de la Septant ", *RB* (1953), LX, p. 18 seq.

Barthélemy, D., and Milik, J. T., *Discoveries in the Judean Desert. I : Qumran, Cave I*, 1955.

Baumgartner, W., " Neue Handschriftenfunde am Toten Meer ", *Archiv für Orientforschung* (1954), XVI, p. 379 seq.

Birnbaum, S. A., " The Date of the Isaiah Scroll ", *BASOR* (1949), No. 113, p. 32 f.

" The Date of the Covenant Scroll ", *PEQ* (1949), LXXXI, p. 140 seq.

" The Leviticus Fragments from the Cave ", *BASOR* (1950), No. 118, p. 20 seq.

Birnbaum, S. A., " Notes on the Internal and Archaeological Evidence Concerning the Cave Scrolls ", *JBL* (1951), LXX, p. 227 seq.
The Qumrân (Dead Sea) Scrolls and Palaeography (*BASOR* Suppl. Stud. Nos. 13–14), 1952.

Brownlee, W. H., " The Jerusalem Habakkuk Scroll ", *BASOR* (1948), No. 112, p. 8 seq.
" A Comparison of the Covenanters of the Dead Sea Scrolls with pre-Christian Jewish Sects ", *BA* (1950), XIII, No. 3, p. 50 seq.
" Excerpts from the Translation of the Dead Sea Manual of Discipline ", *BASOR* (1951), No. 121, p. 8 seq.
The Dead Sea Manual of Discipline (*BASOR* Suppl. Stud. Nos. 10–12), 1951.
" Emendations of the Dead Sea Manual of Discipline and Some Notes Concerning the Habakkuk Midrash ", *JQR* (1954–5), XLV, pp. 141 seq., 198 seq.
" John the Baptist in the New Light of Ancient Scrolls ", *Interpretation* (1955), IX, p. 71 seq.

Bruce, F. F., *Second Thoughts on the Dead Sea Scrolls*, 1956.

Burrows, M., " Variant Readings in the Isaiah Manuscript ", *BASOR* (1948), No. 111, p. 16 seq. ; *BASOR* (1949), No. 113, p. 24 seq.
" Orthography, Morphology and Syntax of the St. Mark's Isaiah Manuscript ", *JBL* (1949), LXVIII, p. 195 seq.
" The Dating of the Dead Sea Scrolls ", *BASOR* (1951), No. 122, p. 4 f.
" Concerning the Dead Sea Scrolls : a reply to Professor Zeitlin ", *JQR* (1951–2), XLII, p. 105 seq.

Burrows, M., Trever, J. C., and Brownlee, W. H., *The Dead Sea Scrolls of St. Mark's Monastery, I : The Isaiah Manuscript and the Habakkuk Commentary*, 1950 ; II, Fasc. 2, *Plates and Transcription of the Manual of Discipline*, 1951.

Burrows, M., *The Dead Sea Scrolls*, 1955.
More Light on the Dead Sea Scrolls, 1958.

Charles, R. H., *Fragments of a Zadokite Work in APOT* (1913), II, p. 785 seq.

Collier, D., " New Radio-carbon Method of Dating the Past ", *BA* (1951), XIV, No. 1, p. 25 seq.

Coppens, J., " Découverte de Nouveaux Manuscrits de la Bible ", *Ephemerides Theologicae Lovanienses* (1949), XXV, p. 309 seq.

Cross, F. M., " The Newly Discovered Scrolls in the Hebrew University Museum in Jerusalem ", *BA* (1949), XII, No. 2, p. 36 seq.

" A New Qumrân Biblical Fragment related to the Original Hebrew underlying the Septuagint ", *BASOR* (1953), No. 132, p. 15 seq.

"The Manuscripts of the Dead Sea Caves ", *BA* (1954), XVII, No. 1, p. 2 seq.

The Ancient Library of Qumran, 1958.

Cullmann, O., " The Significance of the Qumran Texts for Research into the Beginnings of Christianity ", *JBL* (1955), LXXIV, p. 213 seq.

Davies, A. P., *The Meaning of the Dead Sea Scrolls*, 1956.

Delcor, M., " *Les Manuscrits de la Mer Morte : Essai sur le Midrash d'Habacuc* " (Lectio Divina No. 7), 1951.

" Le Midrash d'Habacuc ", *RB* (1951), LVIII, p. 521 seq.

del Medico, H. E., *Deux Manuscrits hébreux de la Mer Morte : essai de traduction du 'Manuel de Discipline' et du ' Commentaire d'Habbakuk ', avec notes et commentaires*, 1951.

de Vaux, R., " Fouille au Khirbet Qumran ", *RB* (1953), LX, p. 83 seq.

" Les Grottes de Murabba'at et leurs documents ", *ibid.* (1953), LX p. 245 seq.

" Exploration de la region de Qumran ", *RB* (1953), LX, p. 540 seq.

" Fouilles au Khirbet Qumran ", *RB* (1954), LXI, p. 206 seq.

Driver, G. R., " New Hebrew Manuscripts ", *JQR* (1949–50), XL, pp. 127 seq., 359 seq.

" New Hebrew Scrolls ", *The Hibbert Journal* (1950), p. 11 seq.

"Hebrew Scrolls ", *Journal of Theological Studies* (1951), II, p. 17 seq.

The Hebrew Scrolls from the Neighbourhood of Jericho and the Dead Sea, 1951.

Dupont-Sommer, A., *Observations sur le Commentaire d'Habacuc découvert près de la Mer Morte*, 1950.

" La 'Règle' de la Communauté de la Nouvelle Alliance ", *Revue de l'Histoire des Religions* (1950), CXXXVIII, p. 5 seq.

Aperçus préliminaires sur les manuscrits de la Mer Morte, 1950 (English translation, *The Dead Sea Scrolls*, by E. M. Rowley, 1952).

Observations sur le Manuel de Discipline découvert près de la Mer Morte, 1951.

Nouveau aperçus sur les Manuscrits de la Mer Morte, 1953 (English translation, *The Jewish Sect of Qumran and the Essenes*, New Studies on the Dead Sea Scrolls, by R. D. Barnett, 1954).

" Quelques remarkes sur le Commentaire d'Habacuc, à propos d'un livre récent ", *VT* (1955), V, p. 113 seq.

Eisler, R., " Hebrew Scrolls : Further Evidence for their pre-Christian Date ", *The Modern Churchman* (1949), XXXIX, p. 284 seq.

Eissfeldt, O., " Varienten der Jesaia-Rolle ", *Theologische Literaturzeiung* (1949), LXXIV, cols. 221 seq.

" Die Bestimmung der aramäisch geschriebenen Rolle als das apokryphe Lamech-Buck ", *ibid.* (1950), LXXV, cols. 23 seq.

Variae lectiones rotulorum manuscriptorum anno 1947 prope Mare Mortuum repertorum ad Jes 1–66 et Hab 1–2 pertinentes, 1951.

Elliger, K., *Studien zum Habakuk-Kommentar vom Toten Meer* (Beiträge zur historischen Theologie, No. 15), 1953.

Fritsch, C. T., " Herod the Great and the Qumran Community ", *JBL* (1955), LXXIV, p. 173 seq.

The Qumran Community, 1956.

Gaster, T. H., *The Dead Sea Scriptures in English Translation*, 1956.

Ginsberg, H. L., " The Hebrew University Scrolls from the Sectarian Cache ", *BASOR* (1948), No. 112, p. 19 seq.

" Notes on the Two Published Letters to Joshua Ben Galgolah ", *BASOR* (1953), No. 131, p. 25 f.

Goosens, R., " L'état actuel des recherches sur les manuscrits de la Mer Morte et sur la secte de la Nouvelle-Alliance ", *La Nouvelle Clio* (1949–50), I–II, p. 634 seq.

" Du Nouveau sur les origines chrétiennes ", *Le Flambeau* (1951), XXXIV, p. 31 seq.

Gottstein, M. H., " Biblical Quotations in the Dead Sea Scrolls ", *VT* (1953), III, p. 79 seq.

" Anti-Essene Traits in the Dead Sea Scrolls ", *VT* (1954), IV, p. 141 seq.

Harding, G. L., " Khirbet Qumran and Wadi Murabba'at ", *PEQ* (1952), LXXXIV, p. 104 seq.

Howlett, D., *The Essenes and Christianity*, 1957.

Kahle, P., " The Karaites and the Manuscript from the Cave ", *VT* (1953), III, p. 82 f.

Kelso, J. L., " The Archeology of Qumran ", *JBL* (1955), LXXIV, p. 141 seq.

Kuhn, K. G., " Die Sektenschrift und die Iranische Religion ", *Zeitschrift für Theologie und Kirche* (1952), XLIX, p. 296 seq.

" Les Rouleaux de cuivre de Qumran ", *RB* (1954), LXI, p. 193 seq.

" Die beiden Messias Aarons und Israels ", *New Testament Studies* (1955), I, p. 168 seq.

Lacheman, E. R., " A Matter of Method in Hebrew Palaeography ", *JQR* (1949–50), XL, p. 15 seq.

" Can Hebrew Palaeography be called ' scientific ' ? ", *JQR* (1951–2), XLII, p. 377 seq.

Loewinger, S., " The Variants of DSI II ", *VT* (1954), IV, p. 155 seq.

Marcus, R., " Pharisees, Essenes and Gnostics ", *JBL* (1954), LXXIII, p. 157 seq.

Martin, W. J., *The Dead Sea Scroll of Isaiah*, 1954.

Michel, A., *Le Maître de Justice*, 1954.

Milik, J. T., " Une Inscription et une lettre en araméen Christo-palestinien ", *RB* (1953), LX, p. 526 seq.

" Un contrat juif de l'an 134 après Jésus Christ ", *RB* (1954), LXI, p. 182 seq.

" Note additionelle sur le contrat juif de l'an 134 aprè Jésus Christ ", *RB* (1955), LXII, p. 253 seq.

Mowry, L., " The Dead Sea Scrolls and the Background for the Gospel of John ", *BA* (1954), XVII, No. 4, p. 78 seq.

Muilenburg, J., " A Qoheleth Scroll from Qumrân ", *BASOR* (1954), No. 135, p. 20 seq.

" Fragments of Another Qumrân Isaiah Scroll ", *BASOR* (1954), No. 135, p. 28 seq.

North, R., " Qumrân and its Archaeology ", *CBQ* (1954), XVI, p. 426 seq.

" The Damascus of Qumrân Geography ", *PEQ* (1955), LXXXVII, pp. 1 seq., 34 seq.

Orlinsky, H. M., " Studies in the St. Mark's Isaiah Scroll, VI ", *Hebrew Union College Annual* (1954), XXV, p. 85 seq.

van der Ploeg, J., " Les Manuscrits du Désert de Juda ", *BO* (1954), XI, p. 145 seq.

Rabin, C., *The Zadokite Documents*, 1954.
" Notes on the Habakkuk Scroll and the Zadokite Document ",
VT (1955), V, p. 148 seq.
Qumran Studies, Scripta Judaica II, 1957.
Rabinowitz, I., " A Hebrew Letter of the Second Century from Beth
Mashko ", *BASOR* (1953), No. 131, p. 21 seq.
" Sequence and Dates of the Extra-Biblical Dead Sea Scroll Texts
and ' Damascus ' Fragments ", *VT* (1953), III, p. 175 seq.
Rabinowitz, J. J., " Note sur la lettre de Bar Kokheba ", *RB* (1954),
LXI, p. 191 f.
" Some Notes on an Aramaic Contract from the Dead Sea Region ",
BASOR (1954), No. 136, p. 15 f.
Reed, W. L., " The Qumran Caves Expedition of March 1952 ",
BASOR (1954), No. 135, p. 8 seq.
Reicke, B., " Die Taʿamire-Schriften und die Damaskus-Fragmente ",
Studia Theologica (1949–50), II, p. 45 seq.
" Traces of Gnosticism in the Dead Sea Scrolls ? ", *New Testament
Studies* (1954), I, p. 137 seq.
" Die Verfassung der Urgemeinde im Lichte jüdischer Dokumente ",
Theologische Zeitschrift (1954), X, p. 95 seq.
Roberts, B. J., " Some Observations on the Damascus Document and
the Dead Sea Scrolls ", *Bulletin of the John Rylands Library* (1952–3),
XXXV.
"The Dead Sea Scrolls and the Old Testament Scriptures ", *ibid.*
(1953–4), XXXVI, p. 75 seq.
" The Qumran Scrolls : A Survey ", *Congregational Quarterly* (1954),
XXXII, p. 114 seq.
Rost, L., " Der ' Lehrer der Einung ' und der ' Lehrer der Gerech-
tigkeit ' ", *Theologische Literaturzeitung* (1953), LXXVIII, cols. 143
seq.
Roth, C., *The Historical Background of the Dead Sea Scrolls*, 1958.
Rowley, H. H., *The Zadokite Fragments and the Dead Sea Scrolls*,
1952.
" The Internal Dating of the Dead Sea Scrolls ", *Ephemerides Theo-
logicae Lovanienses* (1952), XXVIII, p. 257 seq.
The Dead Sea Scrolls and their Significance, 1955.
" The Teacher of Righteousness and the Dead Sea Scrolls ", *Bulletin
of the John Rylands Library* (1957–8), XL, p. 114 seq.

Rubinstein, A., "Notes on the Use of the Tenses and the Variant Readings of the Isaiah Scroll ", *VT* (1953), III, p. 92 seq.

"Isaiah LII iv—MŠḤT—and the DSIa Variant ", *Biblica* (1954), XXXV, p. 475 seq.

"Singularities in Consecutive-Tense Constructions in the Isaiah Scroll ", *VT* (1955), V, p. 180 seq.

"Conditional Constructions in the Isaiah Scroll (DSIa) ", *VT* (1956), VI, p. 69 seq.

Schonfield, H. J., *Secrets of the Dead Sea Scrolls*, 1956.

Scott, R. B. Y., *Treasure from Judean Caves : The Story of the Dead Sea Scrolls*, 1955.

Segal, M. H., "The Promulgation of the Authoritative Text of the Hebrew Bible ", *JBL* (1953), LXXII, p. 35 seq.

Silberman, L. H., "The Two 'Messiahs' of the Manual of Discipline", *VT* (1955), V, p. 77 seq.

Skehan, P. W., "A Fragment of the 'Song of Moses' (Deut. 32) from Qumrân ", *BASOR* (1954), No. 136, p. 12 seq.

"The Text of Isaias at Qumrân ", *CBQ* (1955), XVII, p. 158 seq.

"Exodus in the Samaritan Recension from Qumran ", *JBL* (1955), LXXIV, p. 182 seq.

Sukenik, E. L., *Megilloth Genuzoth*, I (1948) ; II (1950).

"The Scrolls : A reply to Dr. Zeitlin ", *Jewish Chronicle*, November 17th, 1950.

Oṣar ham-Megilloth hag-genuzoth she-bidhe ha-Unibhersitah ha-ʿIbhrith, 1954.

Teicher, J. L., "Method in Hebrew Palaeography ", *JJS* (1951), II, p. 200 f.

"Jesus in the Habakkuk Scroll ", *JJS* (1952), III, p. 53 f.

"The Habakkuk Scroll ", *JJS* (1954), V, p. 47 seq.

"Jesus' Sayings in the Dead Sea Scrolls ", *JJS* (1954), V, p. 38.

"The Christian Interpretation of the Sign X in the Isaiah Scroll ", *VT* (1955), V, p. 189 seq.

"Some Comments on the Palaeography of the Dead Sea Scrolls ", *JJS* (1951), II, p. 195 seq.

Trever, J. C., "Studies in the Problem of Dating the Dead Sea Scrolls ", *Proceedings of the American Philosophical Society* (1953), XCVII, p. 184 seq.

Vermès, G., *Les Manuscrits du Désert de Juda*, 1953.

" Le Cadre historique des manuscrits de la Mer Morte ", Recherches de Science religieuse (1953), XLI, pp. 5 seq., 203 seq.

Discovery in the Judean Desert, 1956.

Wallenstein, M., " Some Lexical Material in the Judean Scrolls ", *VT* (1954), IV, p. 211 seq.

Wernberg-Moeller, P. " Observations on the Interchange of ʿAyin and Ḥeth in the Manual of Discipline ", *VT* (1953), III, p. 104 seq.

" Ṣdq, ṣdyq and ṣdwq in the Zadokite Fragments, the Manual of Discipline and the Habakkuk Commentary ", *VT* (1953), III, p. 310 seq.

Wilson, E., *The Scrolls from the Dead Sea*, 1955.

Yadin, Y., " A Note on DSD, IV, 20 ", *JBL* (1955), LXXIV, p. 40 seq.

The Message of the Scrolls, 1957.

Zeitlin, S., " A Commentary on the Book of Habakkuk : Important Discovery or Hoax ? ", *JQR* (1948–9), XXXIX, p. 235 seq.

" Scholarship and the Hoax of Recent Discoveries ", *JQR*. (1948–9), XXXIX, p. 337 seq.

" The Alleged Antiquity of the Scrolls ", *JQR* (1949–50), XL, p. 57 seq.

" The Hebrew Scrolls : a Challenge to Scholarship ", *JQR* (1950–1), XLI, p. 251 seq.

The Zadokite Fragments : Facsimile of the Manuscripts in the Possession of the University Library, Cambridge, England, 1952.

" Bar Kokba and Bar Kozeba ", *JQR* (1952–3), XLIII, p. 77 seq.

" The Propaganda of the Hebrew Scrolls and the Falsification of History ", *JQR* (1955–6), XLVI, p. 1 seq.

" The Dead Sea Scrolls : Fantasies and Mistranslations ", *JQR* (1957–8), XLVIII, p. 71 seq.

INDEX

Albright, W. F., 6 f., 54
Allegro, J. M., 107
American School of Oriental Research, 6 ff., 31, 34
Assumption of Moses, 27

Barthélemy, D., 47
Biberkraut, J., 37, 39
Book of Enoch, 15, 44, 61, 93
Book of Hagu, 90
Book of Jubilees, 10, 30, 38, 41, 61, 68, 93, 99
Book of Lamech, 38
Book of Noah, 10, 30
Burrows, M., 7, 90

Chalcolithic, 12, 57
Clermont-Ganneau, C., 18, 23 f., 51
Copper scrolls, 14, 42 ff.
Covenanters of Damascus, 87 seq., 91 seq., 97 ff.
Cross, F. M., 28, 124

Damascus document, 44, 87 seq.
Driver, G. R., 58
Dupont-Sommer, A., 74, 99, 102 ff., 107

Ebionites, 100 f.
Ecole Biblique, 3, 17, 41
Essenes, 73 seq., 88, 95 seq., 124

Genesis Apocryphon, 38 ff.
genizah, 4, 16, 87

Habakkuk commentary, 29, 32 ff., 52, 54, 63 f., 66 seq., 88, 90, 98, 120 f.
haburah, 99
Harding, G. L., 2, 4, 7 ff., 14, 17, 19, 42
Hippolytus, 83 ff.

Isaiah scrolls: 1QISa; 6, 29, 31 f., 34, 36, 62 ff., 116; 1QISb; 4 ff., 29, 31

Johannine theology, 110 ff.
John the Baptist, 108 ff.
Josephus, 78 f., 82 f., 96, 98, 116

Karaites, 99 f.
Khirbeh, 17 seq., 22 f.
Khirbet Mird, 47 f.
Khirbet Qumran, 10, 13, 15 ff., 18, 23, 26, 57
Kirkisani, 99 f.
Kittim, 33 f., 53, 67 ff., 98

Magharians, 99 f.

Manual of Discipline, *see* Rule of the Community
Messianic *testimonia*, 105, 120
Milik, J. T., 45, 70
Military scroll, 5, 29, 39, 53 f., 61, 94, 97 f.

Nash papyrus, 6 f.

peshers, 10, 30, 52
Pharisees, 72 f., 99
Philo, 74, 77 f., 83, 85, 97 ff.
Pliny, 73 seq.
Ploeg, J. P. M. van der, 3

Qumran caves: 1Q: 3, 9, 17 f., 22, 24, 26 f., 29 f., 40 f., 51 f., 54, 56, 69, 100; 2Q: 13 f., 41, 56, 64; 3Q: 14, 17, 41 f., 56; 4Q: 15, 44, 87, 105; 5Q: 16; 6Q: 45, 87, 100; 11Q: 45
Qumran sect, 18, 20 f., 24, 34 f., 65 seq., 93 seq., 102 seq.

Radiocarbon dating, 55 f.
Righteous Teacher, 37, 65 ff., 91 f., 98, 102 seq., 107, 120
Rule of the Community, 29, 34 f., 44, 53, 61, 64, 87 seq., 101, 105 f., 110 seq., 122

Saad, J., 9, 11
Sacramental meal, 114, 116 ff.
Sadducees, 72 f., 91, 99
Samuel, Yeshue, *see* Syrian Metropolitan
Scrolls designation, 29
Simon Bar-Kokhba, 13, 46
Sukenik, E. L., 4 seq., 10, 29, 31, 49, 54
Syrian Metropolitan, 3 ff., 8, 24 f., 37, 40

Ta'amireh Bedouin, 2, 9 ff., 13, 29
Testament of Levi, 10, 15, 30, 44, 61
Thanksgiving Hymns, 5, 29, 35 ff., 33 f., 61
Therapeutae, 94
Trever, J. C., 6, 38, 54

Vaux, R. de, 9, 11, 13, 17, 19, 58
Vermès, G., 99

Wadi Murabba'at, 11, 13 ff., 16, 47 f., 57
Wadi Murabba'at caves; 1MU: 58; 2Mu: 45 ff., 58
Wadi Qumran, 2, 10 f.
Wilson, E., 103 f.

Yadin, Y., 25

Zadok, 72, 87
Zadokite document, 16, 53, 87 seq.

haRpeR ⚡ coRchbooks

HUMANITIES AND SOCIAL SCIENCES

American Studies

JOHN R. ALDEN: The American Revolution, 1775-1783.† *Illus.* TB/3011

RAY STANNARD BAKER: Following the Color Line: American Negro Citizenship in the Progressive Era.‡ *Illus. Edited by Dewey W. Grantham, Jr.* TB/3053

RAY A. BILLINGTON: The Far Western Frontier, 1830-1860.† *Illus.* TB/3012

JOSEPH L. BLAU, Ed.: Cornerstones of Religious Freedom in America. *Selected Basic Documents, Court Decisions and Public Statements. Enlarged and revised edition with new Intro. by Editor* TB/118

RANDOLPH S. BOURNE: War and the Intellectuals: Collected Essays, 1915-1919.‡ *Edited by Carl Resek* TB/3043

A. RUSSELL BUCHANAN: The United States and World War II. † *Illus.* Volume I TB/3044 Volume II TB/3045

ABRAHAM CAHAN: The Rise of David Levinsky: a novel. *Introduction by John Higham* TB/1028

JOSEPH CHARLES: The Origins of the American Party System TB/1049

THOMAS C. COCHRAN: The Inner Revolution: Essays on the Social Sciences in History TB/1140

T. C. COCHRAN & WILLIAM MILLER: The Age of Enterprise: A Social History of Industrial America TB/1054

EDWARD S. CORWIN: American Constitutional History: Essays edited by Alpheus T. Mason and Gerald Garvey TB/1136

FOSTER RHEA DULLES: America's Rise to World Power, 1898-1954.† *Illus.* TB/3021

W. A. DUNNING: Reconstruction, Political and Economic, 1865-1877 TB/1073

A. HUNTER DUPREE: Science in the Federal Government: A History of Policies and Activities to 1940 TB/573

CLEMENT EATON: The Growth of Southern Civilization, 1790-1860.† *Illus.* TB/3040

HAROLD U. FAULKNER: Politics, Reform and Expansion, 1890-1900.† *Illus.* TB/3020

LOUIS FILLER: The Crusade against Slavery, 1830-1860.† *Illus.* TB/3029

EDITORS OF FORTUNE: America in the Sixties: the Economy and the Society. *Two-color charts* TB/1015

LAWRENCE HENRY GIPSON: The Coming of the Revolution, 1763-1775.† *Illus.* TB/3007

FRANCIS J. GRUND: Aristocracy in America: Jacksonian Democracy TB/1001

ALEXANDER HAMILTON: The Reports of Alexander Hamilton.‡ *Edited by Jacob E. Cooke* TB/3060

OSCAR HANDLIN, Editor: This Was America: As Recorded by European Travelers to the Western Shore in the Eighteenth, Nineteenth, and Twentieth Centuries. *Illus.* TB/1119

MARCUS LEE HANSEN: The Atlantic Migration: 1607-1860. *Edited by Arthur M. Schlesinger; Introduction by Oscar Handlin* TB/1052

MARCUS LEE HANSEN: The Immigrant in American History. *Edited with a Foreword by Arthur Schlesinger, Sr.* TB/1120

JOHN D. HICKS: Republican Ascendancy, 1921-1933.† *Illus.* TB/3041

JOHN HIGHAM, Ed.: The Reconstruction of American History TB/1068

DANIEL R. HUNDLEY: Social Relations in our Southern States.‡ *Edited by William R. Taylor* TB/3058

ROBERT H. JACKSON: The Supreme Court in the American System of Government TB/1106

THOMAS JEFFERSON: Notes on the State of Virginia.‡ *Edited by Thomas Perkins Abernethy* TB/3052

WILLIAM L. LANGER & S. EVERETT GLEASON: The Challenge to Isolation: The World Crisis of 1937-1940 and American Foreign Policy Volume I TB/3054 Volume II TB/3055

WILLIAM E. LEUCHTENBURG: Franklin D. Roosevelt and the New Deal, 1932-1940.† *Illus.* TB/3025

LEONARD W. LEVY: Freedom of Speech and Press in Early American History: Legacy of Suppression TB/1109

ARTHUR S. LINK: Woodrow Wilson and the Progressive Era, 1910-1917.† *Illus.* TB/3023

ROBERT GREEN McCLOSKEY: American Conservatism in the Age of Enterprise, 1865-1910 TB/1137

BERNARD MAYO: Myths and Men: Patrick Henry, George Washington, Thomas Jefferson TB/1108

JOHN C. MILLER: Alexander Hamilton and the Growth of the New Nation TB/3057

JOHN C. MILLER: The Federalist Era, 1789-1801.† *Illus.* TB/3027

---

† The New American Nation Series, edited by Henry Steele Commager and Richard B. Morris.

‡ American Perspectives series, edited by Bernard Wishy and William E. Leuchtenburg.

* The Rise of Modern Europe series, edited by William L. Langer.

❙ Researches in the Social, Cultural, and Behavioral Sciences, edited by Benjamin Nelson.

§ The Library of Religion and Culture, edited by Benjamin Nelson.

Σ Harper Modern Science Series, edited by James R. Newman.

⁰ Not for sale in Canada.

History: Modern European

FREDERICK B. ARTZ: Reaction and Revolution, 1815-1832.* Illus.   TB/3034
MAX BELOFF: The Age of Absolutism, 1660-1815
                                                                                           TB/1062
ROBERT C. BINKLEY: Realism and Nationalism, 1852-1871.* Illus.   TB/3038
CRANE BRINTON: A Decade of Revolution, 1789-1799.* Illus.   TB/3018
J. BRONOWSKI & BRUCE MAZLISH: The Western Intellectual Tradition: From Leonardo to Hegel
                                                                                           TB/3001
GEOFFREY BRUUN: Europe and the French Imperium, 1799-1814.* Illus.   TB/3033
ALAN BULLOCK: Hitler, A Study in Tyranny.º Illus.
                                                                                           TB/1123
E. H. CARR: The Twenty Years' Crisis, 1919-1939: An Introduction to the Study of International Relationsº
                                                                                           TB/1122
WALTER L. DORN: Competition for Empire, 1740-1763.* Illus.   TB/3032
CARL J. FRIEDRICH: The Age of the Baroque, 1610-1660.* Illus.   TB/3004
LEO GERSHOY: From Despotism to Revolution, 1763-1789.* Illus.   TB/3017
ALBERT GOODWIN: The French Revolution   TB/1064
CARLTON J. H. HAYES: A Generation of Materialism, 1871-1900.* Illus.   TB/3039
J. H. HEXTER: Reappraisals in History: New Views on History and Society in Early Modern Europe
                                                                                           TB/1100
A. R. HUMPHREYS: The Augustan World: Society, Thought, and Letters in Eighteenth Century England
                                                                                           TB/1105
HANS KOHN, Ed.: The Mind of Modern Russia: Historical and Political Thought of Russia's Great Age
                                                                                           TB/1065
SIR LEWIS NAMIER: Vanished Supremacies: Essays on European History, 1812-1918º   TB/1088
JOHN U. NEF: Western Civilization Since the Renaissance: Peace, War, Industry, and the Arts   TB/1113
FREDERICK L. NUSSBAUM: The Triumph of Science and Reason, 1660-1685.* Illus.   TB/3009
RAYMOND W. POSTGATE, Ed.: Revolution from 1789 to 1906: Selected Documents   TB/1063
PENFIELD ROBERTS: The Quest for Security, 1715-1740.* Illus.   TB/3016
PRISCILLA ROBERTSON: Revolutions of 1848: A Social History   TB/1025
ALBERT SOREL: Europe Under the Old Regime. Translated by Francis H. Herrick   TB/1121
N. N. SUKHANOV: The Russian Revolution, 1917: Eyewitness Account. Edited by Joel Carmichael
                                                                           Volume I TB/1066
                                                                           Volume II TB/1067
JOHN B. WOLF: The Emergence of the Great Powers, 1685-1715.* Illus.   TB/3010
JOHN B. WOLF: France: 1814-1919: The Rise of a Liberal-Democratic Society   TB/3019

Intellectual History

HERSCHEL BAKER: The Image of Man: A Study of the Idea of Human Dignity in Classical Antiquity, the Middle Ages, and the Renaissance   TB/1047
J. BRONOWSKI & BRUCE MAZLISH: The Western Intellectual Tradition: From Leonardo to Hegel
                                                                                           TB/3001

ERNST CASSIRER: The Individual and the Cosmos in Renaissance Philosophy. Translated with an Introduction by Mario Domandi   TB/1097
NORMAN COHN: The Pursuit of the Millennium: Revolutionary Messianism in medieval and Reformation Europe and its bearing on modern Leftist and Rightist totalitarian movements   TB/1037
ARTHUR O. LOVEJOY: The Great Chain of Being: A Study of the History of an Idea   TB/1009
ROBERT PAYNE: Hubris: A Study of Pride. Foreword by Sir Herbert Read   TB/1031
BRUNO SNELL: The Discovery of the Mind: The Greek Origins of European Thought   TB/1018
ERNST LEE TUVESON: Millennium and Utopia: A Study in the Background of the Idea of Progress.¶ New Preface by Author   TB/1134

Literature, Poetry, The Novel & Criticism

JAMES BAIRD: Ishmael: The Art of Melville in the Contexts of International Primitivism   TB/1023
JACQUES BARZUN: The House of Intellect   TB/1051
W. J. BATE: From Classic to Romantic: Premises of Taste in Eighteenth Century England   TB/1036
RACHEL BESPALOFF: On the Iliad   TB/2006
R. P. BLACKMUR, et al.: Lectures in Criticism. Introduction by Huntington Cairns   TB/2003
ABRAHAM CAHAN: The Rise of David Levinsky: a novel. Introduction by John Higham   TB/1028
ERNST R. CURTIUS: European Literature and the Latin Middle Ages   TB/2015
GEORGE ELIOT: Daniel Deronda: a novel. Introduction by F. R. Leavis   TB/1039
ETIENNE GILSON: Dante and Philosophy   TB/1089
ALFRED HARBAGE: As They Liked It: A Study of Shakespeare's Moral Artistry   TB/1035
STANLEY R. HOPPER, Ed.: Spiritual Problems in Contemporary Literature§   TB/21
A. R. HUMPHREYS: The Augustan World: Society, ·Thought, and Letters in Eighteenth Century Englandº
                                                                                           TB/1105
ALDOUS HUXLEY: Antic Hay & The Gioconda Smile.º Introduction by Martin Green   TB/3503
ALDOUS HUXLEY: Brave New World & Brave New World Revisited.º Introduction by C. P. Snow
                                                                                           TB/3501
ALDOUS HUXLEY: Point Counter Point.º Introduction by C. P. Snow   TB/3502
HENRY JAMES: The Princess Casamassima: a novel. Introduction by Clinton F. Oliver   TB/1005
HENRY JAMES: Roderick Hudson: a novel. Introduction by Leon Edel   TB/1016
HENRY JAMES: The Tragic Muse: a novel. Introduction by Leon Edel   TB/1017
ARNOLD KETTLE: An Introduction to the English Novel. Volume I: Defoe to George Eliot   TB/1011
Volume II: Henry James to the Present   TB/1012
JOHN STUART MILL: On Bentham and Coleridge. Introduction by F. R. Leavis   TB/1070
PERRY MILLER & T. H. JOHNSON, Editors: The Puritans: A Sourcebook of Their Writings
                                                                           Volume I TB/1093
                                                                           Volume II TB/1094
KENNETH B. MURDOCK: Literature and Theology in Colonial New England   TB/99
SAMUEL PEPYS: The Diary of Samuel Pepys.º Edited by O. F. Morshead. Illustrations by Ernest Shepard
                                                                                           TB/1007

ST.-JOHN PERSE: Seamarks TB/2002
O. E. RÖLVAAG: Giants in the Earth. *Introduction by Einar Haugen* TB/3504
GEORGE SANTAYANA: Interpretations of Poetry and Religion§ TB/9
C. P. SNOW: Time of Hope: *a novel* TB/1040
DOROTHY VAN GHENT: The English Novel: *Form and Function* TB/1050
E. B. WHITE: One Man's Meat. *Introduction by Walter Blair* TB/3505
MORTON DAUWEN ZABEL, Editor: Literary Opinion in America Volume I TB/3013
Volume II TB/3014

Myth, Symbol & Folklore

JOSEPH CAMPBELL, Editor: Pagan and Christian Mysteries. *Illus.* TB/2013
MIRCEA ELIADE: Cosmos and History: *The Myth of the Eternal Return*§ TB/2050
C. G. JUNG & C. KERÉNYI: Essays on a Science of Mythology: *The Myths of the Divine Child and the Divine Maiden* TB/2014
ERWIN PANOFSKY: Studies in Iconology: *Humanistic Themes in the Art of the Renaissance. 180 illustrations* TB/1077
JEAN SEZNEC: The Survival of the Pagan Gods: *The Mythological Tradition and its Place in Renaissance Humanism and Art. 108 illustrations* TB/2004
HELLMUT WILHELM: Change: *Eight Lectures on the I Ching* TB/2019
HEINRICH ZIMMER: Myths and Symbols in Indian Art and Civilization. *70 illustrations* TB/2005

Philosophy

HENRI BERGSON: Time and Free Will: *An Essay on the Immediate Data of Consciousness*° TB/1021
H. J. BLACKHAM: Six Existentialist Thinkers: *Kierkegaard, Nietzsche, Jaspers, Marcel, Heidegger, Sartre*° TB/1002
ERNST CASSIRER: Rousseau, Kant and Goethe. *Introduction by Peter Gay* TB/1092
FREDERICK COPLESTON: Medieval Philosophy° TB/76
F. M. CORNFORD: From Religion to Philosophy: *A Study in the Origins of Western Speculation*§ TB/20
WILFRID DESAN: The Tragic Finale: *An Essay on the Philosophy of Jean-Paul Sartre* TB/1030
PAUL FRIEDLÄNDER: Plato: *An Introduction* TB/2017
ETIENNE GILSON: Dante and Philosophy TB/1089
WILLIAM CHASE GREENE: Moira: *Fate, Good, and Evil in Greek Thought* TB/1104
W. K. C. GUTHRIE: The Greek Philosophers: *From Thales to Aristotle*° TB/1008
F. H. HEINEMANN: Existentialism and the Modern Predicament TB/28
IMMANUEL KANT: The Doctrine of Virtue, *being Part II of The Metaphysic of Morals. Translated with Notes and Introduction by Mary J. Gregor. Foreword by H. J. Paton* TB/110
IMMANUEL KANT: Lectures on Ethics.§ *Introduction by Lewis W. Beck* TB/105
WILLARD VAN ORMAN QUINE: From a Logical Point of View: *Logico-Philosophical Essays* TB/566

BERTRAND RUSSELL et al.: The Philosophy of Bertrand Russell. *Edited by Paul Arthur Schilpp*
Volume I TB/1095
Volume II TB/1096
L. S. STEBBING: A Modern Introduction to Logic TB/538
ALFRED NORTH WHITEHEAD: Process and Reality: *An Essay in Cosmology* TB/1033
WILHELM WINDELBAND: A History of Philosophy I: *Greek, Roman, Medieval* TB/38
WILHELM WINDELBAND: A History of Philosophy II: *Renaissance, Enlightenment, Modern* TB/39

Philosophy of History

NICOLAS BERDYAEV: The Beginning and the End§ TB/14
NICOLAS BERDYAEV: The Destiny of Man TB/61
WILHELM DILTHEY: Pattern and Meaning in History: *Thoughts on History and Society.*° *Edited with an Introduction by H. P. Rickman* TB/1075
RAYMOND KLIBANSKY & H. J. PATON, Eds.: Philosophy and History: *The Ernst Cassirer Festschrift. Illus.* TB/1115
JOSE ORTEGA Y GASSET: The Modern Theme. *Introduction by Jose Ferrater Mora* TB/1038
KARL R. POPPER: The Poverty of Historicism° TB/1126
W. H. WALSH: Philosophy of History: *An Introduction* TB/1020

Political Science & Government

JEREMY BENTHAM: The Handbook of Political Fallacies: *Introduction by Crane Brinton* TB/1069
KENNETH E. BOULDING: Conflict and Defense: *A General Theory* TB/3024
CRANE BRINTON: English Political Thought in the Nineteenth Century TB/1071
EDWARD S. CORWIN: American Constitutional History: *Essays edited by Alpheus T. Mason and Gerald Garvey* TB/1136
ROBERT DAHL & CHARLES E. LINDBLOM: Politics, Economics, and Welfare: *Planning and Politico-Economic Systems Resolved into Basic Social Processes* TB/3037
JOHN NEVILLE FIGGIS: Political Thought from Gerson to Grotius: *1414-1625: Seven Studies. Introduction by Garrett Mattingly* TB/1032
F. L. GANSHOF: Feudalism TB/1058
G. P. GOOCH: English Democratic Ideas in the Seventeenth Century TB/1006
ROBERT H. JACKSON: The Supreme Court in the American System of Government TB/1106
DAN N. JACOBS, Ed.: The New Communist Manifesto and Related Documents TB/1078
DAN N. JACOBS & HANS BAERWALD, Eds.: Chinese Communism: *Selected Documents* TB/3031
ROBERT GREEN McCLOSKEY: American Conservatism in the Age of Enterprise, 1865-1910 TB/1137
KINGSLEY MARTIN: French Liberal Thought in the Eighteenth Century: *A Study of Political Ideas from Bayle to Condorcet* TB/1114
JOHN STUART MILL: On Bentham and Coleridge. *Introduction by F. R. Leavis* TB/1070
JOHN B. MORRALL: Political Thought in Medieval Times TB/1076

JOHN T. McNEILL: Makers of Christianity: *From Alfred the Great to Schleiermacher*   TB/121

A. C. McGIFFERT: Protestant Thought Before Kant. *Preface by Jaroslav Pelikan*   TB/93

KENNETH B. MURDOCK: Literature and Theology in Colonial New England   TB/99

GORDON RUPP: Luther's Progress to the Diet of Worms⁰   TB/120

Judaic Thought & Literature

MARTIN BUBER: Eclipse of God: *Studies in the Relation Between Religion and Philosophy*   TB/12

MARTIN BUBER: Moses: *The Revelation and the Covenant*   TB/27

MARTIN BUBER: Pointing the Way. *Introduction by Maurice S. Friedman*   TB/103

MARTIN BUBER: The Prophetic Faith   TB/73

MARTIN BUBER: Two Types of Faith: *the interpenetration of Judaism and Christianity*⁰   TB/75

MAURICE S. FRIEDMAN: Martin Buber: *The Life of Dialogue*   TB/64

FLAVIUS JOSEPHUS: The Great Roman-Jewish War, *with The Life of Josephus. Introduction by William R. Farmer*   TB/74

T. J. MEEK: Hebrew Origins   TB/69

Oriental Religions: Far Eastern, Near Eastern

TOR ANDRAE: Mohammed: *The Man and His Faith*   TB/62

EDWARD CONZE: Buddhism: *Its Essence and Development.*⁰ *Foreword by Arthur Waley*   TB/58

EDWARD CONZE, et al., Editors: Buddhist Texts Through the Ages   TB/113

ANANDA COOMARASWAMY: Buddha and the Gospel of Buddhism   TB/119

H. G. CREEL: Confucius and the Chinese Way   TB/63

FRANKLIN EDGERTON, Trans. & Ed.: The Bhagavad Gita   TB/115

SWAMI NIKHILANANDA, Trans. & Ed.: The Upanishads: *A One-Volume Abridgment*   TB/114

HELLMUT WILHELM: Change: *Eight Lectures on the I Ching*   TB/2019

Philosophy of Religion

RUDOLF BULTMANN: History and Eschatology: *The Presence of Eternity*   TB/91

RUDOLF BULTMANN AND FIVE CRITICS: Kerygma and Myth: *A Theological Debate*   TB/80

RUDOLF BULTMANN and KARL KUNDSIN: Form Criticism: *Two Essays on New Testament Research. Translated by Frederick C. Grant*   TB/96

MIRCEA ELIADE: The Sacred and the Profane   TB/81

LUDWIG FEUERBACH: The Essence of Christianity.§ *Introduction by Karl Barth. Foreword by H. Richard Niebuhr*   TB/11

ADOLF HARNACK: What is Christianity?§ *Introduction by Rudolf Bultmann*   TB/17

FRIEDRICH HEGEL: On Christianity: *Early Theological Writings. Edited by Richard Kroner and T. M. Knox*   TB/79

KARL HEIM: Christian Faith and Natural Science   TB/16

IMMANUEL KANT: Religion Within the Limits of Reason Alone.§ *Introduction by Theodore M. Greene and John Silber*   TB/67

PIERRE TEILHARD DE CHARDIN: The Phenomenon of Man⁰   TB/83

Religion, Culture & Society

JOSEPH L. BLAU, Ed.: Cornerstones of Religious Freedom in America: *Selected Basic Documents, Court Decisions and Public Statements. Enlarged and revised edition, with new Introduction by the Editor*   TB/118

C. C. GILLISPIE: Genesis and Geology: *The Decades before Darwin*§   TB/51

BENJAMIN NELSON: Religious Traditions and the Spirit of Capitalism: *From the Church Fathers to Jeremy Bentham*   TB/1130

H. RICHARD NIEBUHR: Christ and Culture   TB/3

H. RICHARD NIEBUHR: The Kingdom of God in America   TB/49

RALPH BARTON PERRY: Puritanism and Democracy   TB/1138

WALTER RAUSCHENBUSCH: Christianity and the Social Crisis.‡ *Edited by Robert D. Cross*   TB/3059

KURT SAMUELSSON: Religion and Economic Action: *A Critique of Max Weber's The Protestant Ethic and the Spirit of Capitalism.*⁰ *Trans. by E. G. French; Ed. with Intro. by D. C. Coleman*   TB/1131

ERNST TROELTSCH: The Social Teaching of the Christian Churches.⁰ *Introduction by H. Richard Niebuhr*
Volume I   TB/71
Volume II   TB/72

Religious Thinkers & Traditions

AUGUSTINE: An Augustine Synthesis. *Edited by Erich Przywara*   TB/35

KARL BARTH: Church Dogmatics: *A Selection. Introduction by H. Gollwitzer; Edited by G. W. Bromiley*   TB/95

KARL BARTH: Dogmatics in Outline   TB/56

KARL BARTH: The Word of God and the Word of Man   TB/13

THOMAS CORBISHLEY, s. J.: Roman Catholicism   TB/112

ADOLF DEISSMANN: Paul: *A Study in Social and Religious History*   TB/15

JOHANNES ECKHART: Meister Eckhart: *A Modern Translation by R. B. Blakney*   TB/8

WINTHROP HUDSON: The Great Tradition of the American Churches   TB/98

SOREN KIERKEGAARD: Edifying Discourses. *Edited with an Introduction by Paul Holmer*   TB/32

SOREN KIERKEGAARD: The Journals of Kierkegaard.⁰ *Edited with an Introduction by Alexander Dru*   TB/52

SOREN KIERKEGAARD: The Point of View for My Work as an Author: *A Report to History.*§ *Preface by Benjamin Nelson*   TB/88

SOREN KIERKEGAARD: The Present Age.§ *Translated and edited by Alexander Dru. Introduction by Walter Kaufmann*   TB/94

SOREN KIERKEGAARD: Purity of Heart. *Translated by Douglas Steere*   TB/4

SOREN KIERKEGAARD: Repetition: *An Essay in Experimental Psychology. Translated with Introduction & Notes by Walter Lowrie*   TB/117

SOREN KIERKEGAARD: Works of Love: *Some Christian Reflections in the Form of Discourses*   TB/122

7

NATURAL SCIENCES
AND MATHEMATICS

Biological Sciences

Chemistry

Geography

History of Science

Mathematics

Philosophy of Science

R. B. BRAITHWAITE: Scientific Explanation TB/515

J. BRONOWSKI: Science and Human Values. *Illus.*
TB/505

ALBERT EINSTEIN: Philosopher-Scientist. *Edited by Paul A. Schilpp* Volume I TB/502
Volume II TB/503

WERNER HEISENBERG: Physics and Philosophy: *The Revolution in Modern Science. Introduction by F. S. C. Northrop* TB/549

JOHN MAYNARD KEYNES: A Treatise on Probability.º *Introduction by N. R. Hanson* TB/557

STEPHEN TOULMIN: Foresight and Understanding: *An Enquiry into the Aims of Science. Foreword by Jacques Barzun* TB/564

STEPHEN TOULMIN: The Philosophy of Science: *An Introduction* TB/513

G. J. WHITROW: The Natural Philosophy of Timeº
TB/563

Physics and Cosmology

DAVID BOHM: Causality and Chance in Modern Physics. *Foreword by Louis de Broglie* TB/536

P. W. BRIDGMAN: The Nature of Thermodynamics
TB/537

A. C. CROMBIE, Ed.: Turning Point in Physics TB/535

C. V. DURELL: Readable Relativity. *Foreword by Freeman J. Dyson* TB/530

ARTHUR EDDINGTON: Space, Time and Gravitation: *An outline of the General Relativity Theory* TB/510

GEORGE GAMOW: Biography of PhysicsΣ TB/567

MAX JAMMER: Concepts of Force: *A Study in the Foundation of Dynamics* TB/550

MAX JAMMER: Concepts of Mass *in Classical and Modern Physics* TB/571

MAX JAMMER: Concepts of Space: *The History of Theories of Space in Physics. Foreword by Albert Einstein* TB/533

EDMUND WHITTAKER: History of the Theories of Aether and Electricity
Volume I: *The Classical Theories* TB/531
Volume II: *The Modern Theories* TB/532

G. J. WHITROW: The Structure and Evolution of the Universe: *An Introduction to Cosmology. Illus.*
TB/504

A LETTER TO THE READER

Overseas, there is considerable belief that we are a country of extreme conservatism and that we cannot accommodate to social change.

Books about America in the hands of readers abroad can help change those ideas.

The U. S. Information Agency cannot, by itself, meet the vast need for books about the United States.

You can help.

Harper Torchbooks provides three packets of books on American history, economics, sociology, literature and politics to help meet the need.

To send a packet of Torchbooks [*] overseas, all you need do is send your check for $7 (which includes cost of shipping) to Harper & Row. The U. S. Information Agency will distribute the books to libraries, schools, and other centers all over the world.

I ask every American to support this program, part of a worldwide BOOKS USA campaign.

I ask you to share in the opportunity to help tell others about America.

EDWARD R. MURROW
Director,
U. S. Information Agency

[*retailing at $10.85 to $12.00]

PACKET I: Twentieth Century America

Dulles/America's Rise to World Power, 1898-1954
Cochran/The American Business System, 1900-1955
Zabel, Editor/Literary Opinion in America (two volumes)
Drucker/The New Society: *The Anatomy of Industrial Order*
Fortune Editors/America in the Sixties: *The Economy and the Society*

PACKET II: American History

Billington/The Far Western Frontier, 1830-1860
Mowry/The Era of Theodore Roosevelt and the
    Birth of Modern America, 1900-1912
Faulkner/Politics, Reform, and Expansion, 1890-1900
Cochran & Miller/The Age of Enterprise: *A Social History of
Industrial America*
Tyler/Freedom's Ferment: *American Social History from the
Revolution to the Civil War*

PACKET III: American History

Hansen/The Atlantic Migration, 1607-1860
Degler/Out of Our Past: *The Forces that Shaped Modern America*
Probst, Editor/The Happy Republic: *A Reader in Tocqueville's America*
Alden/The American Revolution, 1775-1783
Wright/The Cultural Life of the American Colonies, 1607-1763

*Your gift will be acknowledged directly to you by the overseas recipient.
Simply fill out the coupon, detach and mail with your check or money order.*

HARPER & ROW, PUBLISHERS · BOOKS USA DEPT.
49 East 33rd Street, New York 16, N. Y.

Packet I ☐   Packet II ☐   Packet III ☐

Please send the BOOKS USA library packet(s) indicated above, in my
name, to the area checked below. Enclosed is my remittance in the
amount of _____ for _____ packet(s) at $7.00 each.

_____ Africa   _____ Latin America

_____ Far East   _____ Near East

Name_____

Address_____

_____

NOTE: This offer expires December 31, 1966.